Origin Myth of Acoma

And Other Records

By

Matthew Williams Stirling

First published in 1942

Published by Left of Brain Books

Copyright © 2023 Left of Brain Books

ISBN 978-1-396-32622-6

First Edition

All rights reserved. No part of this publication may be reproduced, distributed, or transmitted in any form or by any means, including photocopying, recording, or other electronic or mechanical methods, without the prior written permission of the publisher, except in the case of brief quotations permitted by copyright law. Left of Brain Books is a division of Left Of Brain Onboarding Pty Ltd.

PUBLISHER'S PREFACE

About the Book

"A fascinating academic study of the Acoma Pueblo myth cycle."

(Quote from sacred-texts.com)

About the Author

Matthew Williams Stirling (1896 - 1975)

"Matthew Williams Stirling (1896 - January 23, 1975) was an American ethnologist, archaeologist and later an administrator at several scientific institutions in the field. He is best known for his discoveries relating to the Olmec civilization.

Stirling began his career with extensive ethnological work in the United States, New Guinea and Ecuador, before directing his attention to the Olmec civilization and its possible primacy among the pre-Columbian societies of Mesoamerica. His discovery of, and excavations at, various sites attributed to Olmec culture in the Mexican Gulf Coast region significantly contributed towards a better understanding of the Olmecs and their culture. He then began investigating links between the different civilizations in the region. Apart from his extensive field work and publications, later in his career Stirling proved to be an able administrator of academic and research bodies, who served on directorship boards of a number of scientific organizations."

(Quote from wikipedia.org)

CONTENTS

PUBLISHER'S PREFACE
PREFACE 1
ORIGIN MYTH 3
    ORIGIN MYTH 4
    ORIGIN OF THE EVIL SPIRIT 15
    RULE FOR TRACKING LARGE GAME 28
    FETISHES 30
    WANDERINGS, PART I 33
    WANDERINGS, PART II 37
    WANDERINGS, PART III 41
    WANDERINGS, PART IV 46
    WANDERINGS, PART V 50
    WANDERINGS, PART VI 57
    WANDERINGS, PART VII 61
    WANDERINGS, PART VIII 67
    WANDERINGS, PART IX 74
    WANDERINGS, PART X 76
    WANDERINGS, PART XI 80
    WANDERINGS, PART XII 83
    WANDERINGS, PART XIII 85
    WANDERINGS, PART XIV 90
    WANDERINGS, PART XV 92
    WANDERINGS, PART XVI 94
    WANDERINGS, PART XVII 100
    WANDERINGS, PART XVIII 108
    THE BIRTH OF THE WAR TWINS 110
PRESENT CUSTOMS OF ACOMA 117
    SELECTION OF OFFICERS 118
    KATSINA INITIATION 129
    KOSHARI INITIATION 134
    BIBLIOGRAPHY 137
PLATES 143
    EXPLANATION OF PLATES 144
    PLATE 1 145
    PLATE 2 149
    PLATE 3 150

- PLATE 4 152
- PLATE 5 154
- PLATE 6 157
- PLATE 7 159
- PLATE 8 161
- PLATE 9 163
- PLATE 10 165
- PLATE 11 167
- PLATE 12 169
- PLATE 13 171
- PLATE 14 173
- PLATE 15 175
- PLATE 16 177
- PLATE 17 179

ENDNOTES 180

PREFACE

THE following information was obtained in September and October of 1928 from a group of Pueblo Indians from Acoma and Santa Ana visiting Washington.

The Acoma origin and migration myth is presented as it was learned by the chief informant during his initiation in youth into the Koshari, the group of sacred clowns to whom theoretically all religious secrets are divulged. With this myth, according to Acoma ideology, everything in the culture must harmonize. When new practices are adopted, there is an attempt to fit them into the general scheme, although in recounting the tradition, the informant was careful to differentiate between contemporary practice and what was given in the tradition. Frequently after his dictation, when I would question him to bring out concrete instances, he would say, "It is not done so any more." The tradition is couched in archaic language so that in many places the younger interpreters were unable to translate and the elderly informant would have to explain in modern Acoma phraseology. This may account in part for certain obvious paraphrases of Pueblo or even of merely Indian ways of speaking. Other paraphrases may have been made for the benefit of the White man or as interpretation of Acoma religion by one who is an exceptionally good Catholic and no longer a participant in the ceremonial life of Acoma.

Nevertheless, the rendition does present a coherent picture of the religion in a way not accomplished by the fragments of the Keresan origin myth heretofore recorded. The sequential and comprehensive character of this version has given fresh meaning to various concepts and rituals of Keresan religion.

Dr. C. Daryll Forde, who was in Washington at the time, worked with the writer during the recording of the early part of the myth, a section of which was published by him in Folk-Lore, with my permission. The complete manuscript was also utilized by Dr. Parsons in her monograph on Pueblo Religion.

The illustrations were made in water colors by one of the younger Acoma men, under the direction of the chief informant.

Approximately 70 songs were collected. Some of them were recorded from the chief Acoma informant, but the majority were sung by the Santa Ana man who was looked upon as the best singer of the group. Phonographic recordings were made for the Bureau by Mr. Anthony Wilding and later transcribed by Miss Frances Densmore.

All the material recorded, the songs excepted, has been annotated and generally edited by Dr. Leslie A. White, who for many years has been a student of the Keres. Dr. White's first study of Acoma was published by the Bureau in 1932 and two later studies by Dr. White will be included in Bulletin 136, shortly to go to press. The correlation of all the Acoma information, through bibliographical and other references, adds much to the value of the present publication. We are greatly indebted to Dr. White for his collaboration; also to the late Dr. Elsie, Clews Parsons, who took part in the editing.

M. W S.

ORIGIN MYTH

ORIGIN MYTH

IN the beginning [1] two female human beings were born. These two children were born underground at a place called Shipapu. As they grew up, they began to be aware of each other. There was no light and they could only feel each other. Being in the dark they grew slowly.

After they had grown considerably, a Spirit whom they afterward called Tsichtinako [2] spoke to them, and they found that it would give them nourishment. After they had grown large enough to think for themselves, they spoke to the Spirit when it had come to them one day and asked it to make itself known to them and to say whether it was male or female, but it replied only that it was not allowed to meet with them. They then asked why they were living in the dark without knowing each other by name, but the Spirit answered that they were nuk'timi [3] (under the earth); but they were to be patient in waiting until everything was ready for them to go up into the light. So they waited a long time, and as they grew they learned their language from Tsichtinako.

When all was ready, they found a present from Tsichtinako, two baskets of seeds and little images of all the different animals (there were to be) in the world. The Spirit said they were sent by their father. They asked who was meant by their father, and Tsichtinako replied that his name was Ūch'tsiti [4] and that he wished them to take their baskets out into the light, when the time came. Tsichtinako instructed them, "You will find the seeds of four kinds of pine trees, lā'khok, gēi'etsu (dyai'its), wanūka, and lă'nye, in your baskets. You are to plant these seeds and will use the trees to get up into the light." They could not see the things in their baskets but feeling each object in turn they asked, "Is this it?" until the seeds were found. They then planted the seeds as Tsichtinako instructed. All of the four seeds sprouted, but in the darkness the trees grew very slowly and the two sisters became very anxious to reach the light as they waited this long time. They slept for many years as they had no use for eyes. Each time they awoke they would feel the trees to see how they were growing. The tree lanye grew faster than the others and after a very long time pushed a hole through the earth for them and let in a very little light. The others stopped growing, at various heights, when this happened.

The hole that the tree lanye made was not large enough for them to pass through, so Tsichtinako advised them to look again in their baskets where they would find the image of an animal called dyu·pi (badger) and tell it to become alive. They told it to live, and it did so as they spoke, exclaiming, "A'uha! Why have you given me life?" They told it not to be afraid nor to worry about coming to life. "We have brought you to life because you are to be useful." Tsichtinako spoke to them again, instructing them to tell Badger to climb the pine tree, to bore a hole large enough for them to crawl up, cautioning him not to go out into the light, but to return, when the hole was finished. Badger climbed the tree and after he had dug a hole large enough, returned saying that he had done his work. They thanked him and said, "As a reward you will come up with us to the light and thereafter you will live happily. You will always know how to dig and your home will be in the ground where you will be neither too hot nor too cold."

Tsichtinako now spoke again, telling them to look in the basket for Tāwāi'nū (locust), giving it life and asking it to smooth the hole by plastering. It, too was to be cautioned to return. This they did and Locust smoothed the hole but, having finished, went out into the light. When it returned reporting that it had done its work, they asked it if it had gone out. Locust said no, and every time he was asked he replied no, until the fourth time when he admitted that he had gone out. They asked Locust what it was like outside. Locust replied that it was just tsī'ītī (laid out flat). They said, "From now on you will be known as Tsi·k'ǎ. [5] You will also come up with us, but you will be punished for disobedience by being allowed out only a short time. Your home will be in the ground and you will have to return when the weather is bad. You will soon die but you will be reborn each season."

The hole now let light into the place where the two sisters were, and Tsichtinako spoke to them, "Now is the time you are to go out. You are able to take your baskets with you. In them you will find pollen and sacred corn meal. When you reach the top, you will Wait for the sun to come up and that direction will be called ha'nami (east). With the pollen and the sacred corn meal you will pray to the Sun. You will thank the Sun for bringing you to light, ask for a long life and happiness, and for success in the purpose for which you were created." Tsichtinako then taught them the prayers and the creation song, which they were to sing. This took a long while, but finally the sisters followed by Badger and Locust, went out into the light, climbing the pine tree. Badger was very strong and skillful and helped them. On reaching the earth, they set down their baskets and saw for the first time what they had. The earth was soft and spongy under their feet as they walked, and they said, "This is not ripe." They stood waiting for the sun, not knowing where it would appear. Gradually it grew lighter and finally the sun came up. Before they began to pray, Tsichtinako told them they were facing east and that their right side, the side their best aim was on, would be known as kūʼāimē (South) and the left ti dyami (north) while behind at their backs was the direction pūnaʼme (west) where the sun would go down. They had already learned while underground the direction nŭkʼŭmi (down) and later, when they asked where their father was, they were told tyunami (four skies above.)

And as they waited to pray to the Sun, the girl on the right moved her best hand and was named Iatiku which meant "bringing to life." Tsichtinako then told her to name her sister, but it took a long time. Finally Tsichtinako noticed that the other had more in her basket, so Tsichtinako told Iatiku to name her thus, and Iatiku called her Nautsiti which meant "more of everything in the basket" [6]

They now prayed to the Sun as they had been taught by Tsichtinako, and sang the creation song. Their eyes hurt for they were not accustomed to the strong light. For the first time they asked Tsichtinako why they were on earth and why they were created. Tsichtinako replied, "I did not make you. Your father, Uchtsiti made you, and it is he who has made the world, the sun which you have seen, the sky, and many other things which you will see. But Uchtsiti says the world is not yet completed, not yet satisfactory, as he wants it. This is the reason he has made you. You will rule and bring to life the rest of the things he has given you in the baskets." The sisters then asked how they themselves had come into being. Tsichtinako answered saying, "Uchtsiti first made the world. He threw a clot of his own blood into space and by his power it grew and grew until it became the earth. Then Uchtsiti planted you in this and by it you were nourished as you developed. Now that you have emerged from within the earth, you will have to provide nourishment for yourselves. I will instruct you in this." They then asked where their father lived and Tsichtinako replied, "You will never see your father, he lives four skies above,[7] and has made you to live in this world. He has made you in the image of himself." So they asked why Tsichtinako did not become visible to them, but Tsichtinako replied, "I don't know how to live like a human being. I have been asked by Uchtsiti to look after you and to teach you. I will always guide you." And they asked again how they were to live, whether they could go down once more under the ground, for they were afraid of the winds and rains and their eyes were hurt by the light. Tsichtinako replied that Uchtsiti would take care of that and would furnish them means to keep warm and change the atmosphere so that they would get used to it.

At the end of the first day, when it became dark they were much frightened, for they had not understood that the sun would set and thought that Tsichtinako had betrayed them. "Tsichtinako! Tsichtinako! You told us we were to come into the light," they cried, "why, then, is it dark?" So Tsichtinako explained, "This is the way it will always be. The sun will go down and the next day come up anew in the east. When it is dark you are to rest and sleep as you slept when all was dark." So they were satisfied and slept. They rose to meet the sun, praying to it as they had been told, and were happy when it came up again, for they were warm and their faith in Tsichtinako was restored.

Tsichtinako next said to them, "Now that you have your names, you will pray with your names and your clan names so that the Sun will know you and recognize you." Tsichtinako asked Nautsiti which clan she wished to belong to. Nautsiti answered, "I wish to see the sun, that is the clan I will be." [8]The spirit told Nautsiti to ask Iatiku what clan she wanted. Iatiku thought for a long time but finally she noticed that she had the seed from which sacred meal was made in her basket and no other kind of seeds. She thought, "With this name I shall be very proud, for it has been chosen for nourishment and it is sacred." So she said, "I will be Corn clan." They then waited for the sun to come up. When it appeared, Tsichtinako once more advised them to sing the first song and to pray, not forgetting their name and their clan name in starting their prayer. After the prayer they were to sing the second song.

When the sun appeared it was too bright for Iatiku and it hurt her eyes. She wondered if Nautsiti's eyes hurt her, too, so she put her head down and sideways, letting her hair fall, and looked at Nautsiti.

By doing this the light did not strike her squarely in the face and her hair cast a shade. Tsichtinako said, "Iatiku, the sun has not appeared for you. Look at Nautsiti, see how strongly the light is striking her. Notice how white she looks." And although Iatiku turned to the sun, it did not make her as white as Nautsiti, and Iatiku's mind was slowed up while Nautsiti's mind was made fast. But both of them remembered everything and did everything as they were taught.

When they had completed their prayers to the sun, Tsichtinako said, "You have done everything well and now you are both to take up your baskets and you must look to the north, west, south, and east, for you are now to pray to the Earth to accept the things in the basket and to give them life. First you must pray to the north, at the same time lift up your baskets in that direction. You will then do the same to the west, then to the south and east." They did as they were told and did it well. And Tsichtinako, said to them, "From now on you will rule in every direction, north, west, south, and east."

They now questioned Tsichtinako again so that they would understand more clearly why they were given the baskets and their contents, and Tsichtinako, replied, "Everything in the baskets is to be created by your word, for you are made in the image of Uchtsiti and your word will be as powerful as his word. He has created you to help him complete the world. You are to plant the seeds of the different plants to be used when anything is needed. I shall always be ready to point out to you the various plants and animals."

The sisters did not realize that they were not taking food and did not understand when Tsichtinako told them they were to plant seeds to give them nourishment. But they were always ready to do as Tsichtinako, asked, and she told them to plant first that which would maintain life, grains of corp. "When this plant grows," said Tsichtinako, "it will produce a part which I will point out to you. This will be taken as food." Everything in the basket was in pairs and the sisters planted two of each kind of corn.

The corn grew very slowly so Tsichtinako told them to plant ĭsthĕ (the earliest plant to come up in the spring; gray with a small white flower; dies quickly) and to transmit its power of early ripening to the corn.

They were very interested in the corn and watched it every day as it grew. Tsichtinako showed them where the pollen came out. "That you will call kū'ăch'tīmu," she said, "there the pollen win appear. When the pollen is plentiful, you will gather it, and with it and corn meal you will pray to the rising sun each morning." This they did always, but Nautsiti was sometimes a little lazy.

After some time the corn ripened. Tsichtinako told them to look at it and to gather some. They saw that the corn was hard and they picked four ears. Iatiku took two ears carefully without hurting the plant, but Nautsiti jerked hers off roughly. Iatiku noticed this and cautioned her sister not to ruin the plants. They took the ears of corn to Tsichtinako saying, "We have brought the corn, it is ripe." Tsichtinako agreed and explained that the corn ears when cooked would be their food. They did not understand this and asked what they would cook with. Tsichtinako then told them that Uchtsiti would give them fire. That night as they sat around they saw a red light drop from the sky. After they had seen it, Tsichtinako told them it was fire, and that they were to go over and get some of it. They asked with what, and she told them to get it with a flat rock because it was very hot and they could not take it in their hands. After getting it with a rock, they asked what they were to do with it, and were told they were to make a fire, to go to the pine tree they had planted, to break off some of the branches and put them in the fire. They went to the tree and broke some of the twigs from it. When they got back to the fire, they were told to throw the twigs down. They did so and a large pile of wood appeared there. Tsichtinako told them this wood would last many years till there was time for trees to grow, and showed them how to build a fire. She told them that with the flames from the fire they would keep warm and would cook their food.

Tsichtinako next taught them how to roast the corn. "When it is cooked," she explained, "you are to eat it. This will be the first time you have eaten, for you have been fasting for a long time and Uchtsiti has been nourishing you. You will find salt in your baskets; with this you will season the corn." They began to look for this and Tsichtinako pointed it out to them. As soon as they were told this, Nautsiti grabbed some corn and salt. She was the first to taste them and exclaimed that they were very good, but Iatiku was slower. After Nautsiti had eaten part, she gave it to Iatiku to taste. When both had eaten, Tsichtinako told them that this was the way they were going to live, and be nourished. They were very thankful, saying, "You have treated us well," They asked if this would be their only food. Tsichtinako said, "No, you have many other things in your baskets; many seeds and images of animals, all in pairs. Some will be eaten and taken for nourishment by you." After they had used the salt, they were asked by Tsichtinako to give life to this salt by praying to the Earth, first in the North direction, then in the West, then in the South, and then in the. East. And when they did so, salt appeared in each of these directions. Tsichtinako then instructed them to take always the husks from the corn carefully and to dry them. They were then instructed to plant hă'mi (tobacco). When the plant matured, they were taught how to roll the leaves in corn husks and to smoke it. (Even now in ceremonies the corn husks must be torn with the fingers and tied in the center with a little strip of corn husk. It may not be cut by artificial means. You smoke in order to make your prayers merge into the minds of the gods to whom prayer is addressed. This will also compel obedience. If a man smokes when a request is made of him, he must obey that request.) They were then told to place the tobacco with the pollen and the corn meal and to remember that these three were always to be together, and to be used in making prayers.

Now they were told that they were to give life to an animal whose flesh they were going to use for food. Tsichtinako named this animal as Ba'shya (kangaroo mouse) and also taught them the first song to be sung to animals. She told them to sing this song in order to make the images alive, and pointed out the images to them in the basket.

They did everything as they were taught. They sang the song to the image and with the word, "Come to life, Bashya," it came to life. As it did so it asked, "Why have I come to life?" Tsichtinako told it not to ask any questions because, "It is you that is going to give life to other life." After this was done, Nautsiti and Iatiku, told this animal that it was going to live on the ground and said to it, "Go now and increase." After the animal increased, Tsichtinako told the sisters to kill one of the animals. "Now eat the two together, the corn and the field mouse, and also the salt to see how it tastes." She had already told them never to let out the fire which had been given to them. They acted according to Tsichtinako's instructions. They roasted their corn and roasted the flesh of the field mouse with some salt on it. After it was cooked, Tsichtinako told them to pray with the food, not with all of it, but with little pieces from each--corn, flesh, and salt. Each sister did this and prayed to Uchtsiti, the creator of the world, who lives up in the fourth sky. Tsichtinako told them they were to do this always before eating. After this they ate the food. There was not very much of the meat, but it was good. They did not know that there were to be bones but these were not hard and they broke them with their teeth. They liked the flesh so well that they asked Tsichtinako if they might have something larger that would yield more flesh. Tsichtinako answered that they would find other things in their baskets. They went back to them, and Tsichtinako said they would find Tsū'na [9](rat) and another animal Katsa [10](mole) and also Nīte. [11](prairie dog). "Go, make these images alive," said Tsichtinako, pointing them out according to their names. They were to do this in the same way as with Bashya. Tsichtinako also told them that these animals were to be used as food and that they must tell each of these animals to live in the ground because as yet there was no shade on earth to live in. "But before you give life to them," said Tsichtinako, "it is necessary that you plant seeds of grass which will be the food for them." Tsichtinako pointed out the seeds they were to plant, and they took the seeds of the grasses and scattered them first to the North, next to the West, then some to the South, and then to the East. And immediately grass covered the ground. They then took the images and prayed to the cardinal points, and, according to the instructions of Tsichtinako, gave life to all of these animals, giving them names as they came to life. Each one as it came to life asked why it had come to life but Tsichtinako told them not to ask questions, that they would give life to other life. As before, the sisters told the animals to increase. After all of this was done, they proceeded to eat the new animals after praying with them, doing just as they did before. The two sisters were now very happy, they had plenty and some to spare. "It is not yet time for the larger animals to 'be given life," said Tsichtinako, "first the world must have sufficient plants and small animals to feed them."

After a long time, Tsichtinako spoke to them, "What we are going to do now concerns the earth. We are going to make the mountains." She told them to remember the words she was going to say. They were to say, "Kaweshtima kōti [12](North Mountain), appear in the north, and we will always know you to be in that direction." Tsichtinako also pointed out an article in the basket that she named ya'ōni [13](stone) and instructed them to throw the stone to the North direction as they spoke the words. When they did so,, a big mountain appeared in the North. After they had done this, Tsichtinako instructed them to do the same thing in the West, but to name this mountain Tsipīna koti, and in the South, naming it Da'ōtyuma koti, and in the East, naming it G'ūchana koti.

After all this was done, Tsichtinako spoke again and told them, "Now that you have all the mountains around you with plains, mesas, and canyons, you must make the growing things of these places." Tsichtinako told them to go back to the trees which they had planted underground, lakhok, geietsu, wanuka, and lanye. She told them to take the seeds from these trees, and they did so. Following her instructions they spread some to each of the four directions, naming the mountains in each direction, and saying, "Grow in North Mountain, grow in West Mountain, etc." Tsichtinako said to them, "These are going to be tall trees; from them you will get logs. Later you will build houses and will use these." They asked if that was all that was going to grow on the mountains, and Tsichtinako said, "No, there are many other seeds left in your baskets. You have seeds of trees which are going to yield food. You will find dyai'its [14](piñon tree), sē'isha (kind of cedar), hapani (oak, acorn) and maka'yawi (walnut)." She again instructed them what to do and taught them the prayer to use, which was: "From now on, grow in this mountain and yield fruit which will be used as food. Your places are to be in the mountains. You will grow and be useful." When everything had been done well, Tsichtinako told (them) that there were many smaller seeds left in the baskets and she gave a name to each, telling them to fill the rest of the land. These seeds were planted on every one of the four mountains and in the rest of the world. Tsichtinako spoke to the sisters again and told them, "You still have seeds in your baskets which you will know as scuts'ōibewi (wild fruits). These trees you will grow around you and care for." But they mistook the instructions and instead of instructing them to grow nearby, they named the mountains, and that is where they grew. But there were also some that grew close around. It is not known how long they had to wait for these things to happen, but it was a very long time. They noticed that the wild plants grew very fast and produced much fruit, but Tsichtinako had not told them whether or not to eat these, so they left them alone.

They saw that there were still seeds and images in their baskets, and asked Tsichtinako how many more kinds there were. Tsichtinako, said there were yet many other seeds which would also be important food. They would grow quickly and easily and she named them squash and beans. They were instructed to act with them as with the other seeds, and these also grew into plants. After a time, when they were ripe, Tsichtinako pointed out the parts of the plants which they, were to use as food.

Iatiku later asked Tsichtinako, "What remains in my basket?" and she was answered, "You have still many animals; these will be multiplied to populate the mountains." And as the two grew larger, they required more food. Tsichtinako saw this and told them that they were now to bring to life larger animals. She said they would find in their baskets cottontails, jack rabbits, antelope, and water deer. They were told to give life to these animals and to send them into the open plains. Everything was done as before, and when they killed the animals for food they were always careful to pray to their father as before. As they again asked Tsichtinako what remained in their baskets, Tsichtinako said, "You have images of the still bigger game. You will find deer, elk, mountain sheep, and bison." Iatiku asked where these animals were to be told to live and Tsichtinako told them that the elk and deer were to live in the lower mountains and the mountain sheep higher and in the rougher places. The bison, however, were to live on the plains. They followed the instructions and gave life to these animals and told them to go to these places to live and multiply. They again tried all these different animals for food. Their flesh was very good and always they prayed to Uchtsiti before tasting them.

In Nautsiti's basket there were many more things left than in Iatiku's. Nautsiti was selfish and hoarded her images, but Iatiku was ready to let her seeds and images be used. She was more interested in seeing things grow. They again asked what remained, and Tsichtinako replied, "You will find lion, wolf, wildcat and bear. These are strong beasts; they are going to use as food the same game that you also use. There is now game enough for them." When all these had been selected they were brought to life in the same manner as before.

The sisters again asked what was in their baskets, and they were told, "You will find birds which will fly in the air. These birds win also use small game for their food. You will find in the basket the eagles and the hawks (shpi·ya, [15]ga·wa, [16]i·tsa)." [17]Tsichtinako pointed these out to them and they brought them to life. The birds flew up into the high mountains and over the plains. The sisters told the birds to use small game for food, and again Iatiku asked what was in the basket. Tsichtinako pointed out smaller birds which would populate the country, each living in a different kind of region. They were then given life, as the animals before them. The birds were of many and bright colors, some were blue. The wild turkey was among them and they were instructed to tell it not to fly easily like the others. They were told to tell these birds that their food was to be the different seeds on the mountains and the plains. And all these, animals were sampled for food after they had been given life. Again Iatiku asked what remained in the baskets, because she found things there that were thorny. Tsichtinako told them their names. They were the various cacti and were said to be very good for food. But Tsichtinako explained that most were intended for animals to eat. All these were planted as before and tried for food, and they found that some tasted good, stī'ăne, īcht, ya'tăp, iteō'on. After they asked again what was left, Tsichtinako pointed out to them that there were still fish, water snakes, and turtles, of which there were many kinds of each. They gave life to them as before and told them all to live in the water as instructed. Tsichtinako pointed out several that were to be used for food. They tried them all for food, and they found that some were good, and others poor, but offered prayers to all and gave thanks to Uchtsiti. So it happened that many animals came alive in the world and they all increased.

ORIGIN OF THE EVIL SPIRIT

WHEN Tsichtinako was instructing Iatiku and Nautsiti, Tsichtinako cautioned them to be always very careful in handling their baskets. They were very careful for a while but they soon became too anxious to give life to what was still in their baskets and they became careless. When Iatiku and Nautsiti were giving life to the snakes and fishes, in their eagerness they dropped an image from a basket to the ground. They did not know this had happened, nor did Tsichtinako. The image came to life itself, and with power of its own. It came to life in the form of a serpent, like the rest of the snakes. The two sisters noticed a strange snake among the ones to which they had given life, but they only stopped long enough to ask each other, "Did we give life to that snake?" and paid no more attention to it, as it looked like the others. This was the snake that was to tempt Nautsiti.

Now Nautsiti spoke to Iatiku, who had used more of the seeds and images from her basket, and said she wanted a chance to give life to more of her images. Iatiku replied, "I am the older, you are younger than I," but Nautsiti said, "We should both give equally because we were created equally. Is it true that you are the older? Let us try each other! Tomorrow, when the sun rises, let us see who is going to have the sun rise for her first." But Iatiku was afraid that her sister was going to get the better of her in some way. She knew a white bird that was named shō'ēka [18] (magpie). She went to it and asked it to go on ahead into the east, where the sun was to rise, without resting or eating. There it was to shade the sun with its wings from Nautsiti. The bird went as instructed, for it was very strong and skillful. But, while on its way, it got hungry and it passed a place where a puma had killed a deer. Here, although it had been instructed not to stop, it stopped and found a hole in the side of the deer where the intestines were exposed. The bird put its head into the gash to eat, and as it did so it got blood on its back and wings and tail, and it flew on not noticing that it was stained from the blood. Finally, after a long time, the bird reached the east where the sun was ready to rise and it spread its wings on the left of the sun, making a shade in the direction of Nautsiti. So the sun struck Iatiku first and she straightaway claimed to be the older. And Nautsiti was very angry for she had hoped to win. Iatiku, who did not want her sister to know anything about the trick she had used, whispered to the bird when it returned from the east, telling it not to say anything, and she also punished the bird for disobeying her. She had told it not to stop to eat on the way to the rising sun, but she knew that the bird had stopped for it was all dirty with blood. So she said to it, "For stopping and eating you will not know from now on how to kill your own meat. You will not be a hunter, you will eat what others have killed and left, and most of the time you will eat what is spoiled. Your color also will be spotted from now on, you will not be white as you were at first."

The two sisters were now thinking selfish thoughts. Nautsiti schemed to get the better of her sister. She often wandered off, making plans to outdo Iatiku, but Iatiku watched her and noticed everything. She saw that Nautsiti was falling away from her and was not happy as she used to be. Iatiku also noticed that Nautsiti was becoming solitary and that she would wander off alone. Iatiku tried to comfort her and asked her why she had changed.

A long time before this Tsichtinako had told them that Uchtsiti forbade them to think of having children. In due time other humans made in their likeness would be borne to them. But one day Pishuni, the snake that had come to life of itself, met Nautsiti and said to her, "Why are you lonely and unhappy? If you want what will make you happy, I can tell you what to do. You are the only one on earth that is lonely. You and your sister do not like each other. If you bore someone like yourself, you would no longer be lonely. Tsichtinako, wants to hold back this happiness from you. Unless you do as I tell you, you will have to wait a long time." Nautsiti asked Pishuni how she could do this, and the serpent replied, "Go to the rainbow. He will meet you and show you what to do." Nautsiti thought it would be well to do what Pishuni said. Soon after she was sitting alone on a rock when it rained. It was very hot and the rain steamed on the hot ground. Nautsiti lay on her back to receive the rain, and the dripping water entered her. This was the work of rainbow, and she conceived without knowing what had happened. Some time after, Iatiku noticed that Nautsiti was pregnant. After a time she bore twin sons. Iatiku helped her sister to take care of them. Tsichtinako came back to them and asked, "Why have you done this without my instructing you? Uchtsiti had forbidden you this." Tsichtinako, left them angrily, saying, "From now on, you will do as you see fit. I will not help you any more because you disobeyed your father." But instead of being sorry, the two sisters felt happier. It happened that Nautsiti disliked one of the children. So Iatiku took this one and cared for it.

Because they had committed a sin, their father called Tsichtinako away from them. But they lived happily, and the children grew up. After a long time Nautsiti said to Iatiku, "We are not happy together. Let us share what we have in our baskets and separate. I still have many things. These animals in my basket, these sheep and cattle I will share with you, but it is understood that these animals will demand much care." Iatiku answered that it would be too hard a task to care for them and that she did not want her children to have them. Nautsiti also pointed out some seeds and told Iatiku to take some of them. They were seeds of wheat and vegetables. Nautsiti knew also that these were going to be hard to raise, but she wanted to share them with Iatiku. But Iatiku. again did not want them for her children. In Nautsiti's basket, too, there were many metals. She offered to share these, but Iatiku did not take any. When. Nautsiti had looked this far into her basket she found something written (ti'thyătra'nī). Nautsiti also offered this, but Iatiku did not want it. Nautsiti said, "There are still many things that are very good for foods in my basket but I know that all of these things will require much care. Why is it, sister, that you are not thankful, why do you not take some of the things I have offered? I am going to leave you. We both understand that we are to increase our kind, and in a long time to come we shall meet again and then you will be wearing clothes. We shall still be sisters, for we have the same father, but I shall have the better of you again. I am going away into the East." Iatiku, did not say where she would go. She thought she would stay where she was. So Nautsiti left her, taking the child she loved with her and leaving the other for Iatiku.

So Nautsiti disappeared into the East, while Iatiku stayed on and became very sad. She said to the boy child who stayed with her, "We shall live here with everything that our father has given us." They lived together for a long time and when he grew up, he became her husband and she named him Tia'muni. Iatiku bore many children and she named the first for the clan of her sister--the Sun clan. Now Iatiku had her own power. She did everything in the way she had been instructed; she took the child the fourth day after birth to pray to the sun, as she herself had been taught when she came into the light, and she put some pollen and some sacred corn meal into the child's hands. She taught this to every child that she bore after this. And the brothers and the sisters all lived together and they all began to increase. Iatiku was the mother and ruled.

Whenever a girl was born to Iatiku, she gave it a clan name. The first clan mothers in order of birth were as follows:

Sun clan, oshach hano; named thus because Iatiku was still grieving over Nautsiti who had named herself of the Sun clan.

Sky clan, hoak'ă hano.
Water clan, ts'its hano.
Badger clan, dyupi hano.
Fire clan, hakanyi hano.

After naming these, she thought she would name the rest after things she had brought to life; so the next in order were named:

Antelope clan, ku'uts hano.
Deer clan, diĕhni' hano.[19]
Bear clan, kohaiya [20]hano.

She did not give her own clan name, Yaka hano, Corn clan, as she wanted to be kept apart, so she divided it as follows:

Red corn, kūgănish yaka hano.
Yellow corn, kūŭchnish yaka hano.
Blue corn, kūiskkush yaka hano.
White corn, kăshăish [21]yaka hano.

The next clans in order were:

Oak clan, hapani hano.
Squash clan, tănyi' hano.
Roadrunner clan, shaaskă hano.
Eagle clan, dyami hano.
Turkey clan, tsina hano.
isthe (?) clan, isthe [22]hano.

(These are the only clan names mentioned in the myth, though many other clans later came into existence, as for example the Parrot, Snake, Buffalo, and Ant. These were not descended from daughters of Iatiku.)

Now that Tsichtinako had left her, Iatiku wished for other rulers, so she made the Spirits of the seasons. There was still some earth in her basket. She took this and gave it life in the same way as before. First she made Sha·k'ako, [23] the spirit of Winter (ko·ko) (pl. 3, fig. 2)., To him she said, "You will give life to everything in the winter time. You are to be ugly and ferocious. You will not live with us, go to a distance. You will live in North Mountain, and I shall give you your costume."

Next she gave life to Morityema, the spirit of Spring (ti·cha) (pl. 1, upper left). To him also she gave a costume which was ugly, and she sent him to West Mountain. [24] She next made Maiyochina, the spirit of Summer (kashai'ti), and sent him to South Mountain (pl. 1, upper right). And finally she gave life to Shrui'sthia, [25] the spirit of Fall (haiya'tsi), [26] and sent him to East Mountain (pl. 4, fig. 1). All these creatures were ugly [27] and not in the likeness of the children she had borne. She thought, "Now that I have placed strong rulers in each direction, each will order the earth in turn," and she instructed each one where to work and how. The spirit of Winter she told to bring snow; the spirit of Spring was to warm up the world; the spirit of Summer was to heat the world, giving life to vegetation. The spirit of Fall was not to like the smell of plants and fruits, so he was to work to get rid of the smell by ridding the world of plants. And Iatiku told her children that they were to depend on these spirits and were to pray to them in their various directions, for moisture, warmth, ripening, and frost. She taught them how to pray to the spirits, explaining that each would require certain prayers and prayer sticks before they would answer.

Now when this was done, Iatiku gave life to the other spirits she was going to believe in. With dirt from her basket she gave life to the katsina. The first she named Ts'its'anïts [28] (pl. 1, lower left) (no female was made for this first one); the others as she created them, male and female, she named Kuashtoch [29] (sticking up), so called from feathers on one side of the head (pl. 1, center right); Kuapichani, [30] Divided," so called because one side of his face is yellow and the other red (pl. 5, fig. 1); Wai'osh A full company of Wai'oca appears in dances at Acoma (White, 1932, p. 75, pl. 4, f.). Duck katsina are found in most, if not all Keresan pueblos. [31] (duck), He'mïsh, [32] Na'wish [33] (pl. 6, fig. 1), Kohaiya [34] (bear), Kakuipĕ, [35] Gomaiowish [36] (messenger), Mo·ots, [37] Ahote, and, finally, Cha'koya [38] (pl. 7, fig. 1), who is a great hunter. She called Tsitsanits to her, saying, "I am going to give you your costume. You are very handsome; but you will have a mask which will make you appear different from humans." Iatiku made this mask (shpi·tso) out of buffalo skin. (All masks are of buffalo skin.) She made it to fit the god and then colored it with colors from different earths. She also put different feathers on it. On the head of the god she put this mask and around his neck a wildcat skin. She then painted the god's body and gave him a skirt, belt, and moccasins. She put cords on each wrist and dyed buffalo skins on his arms. On his calves with cords she bound spruce branches. When she had completed this costume Iatiku said to Tsitsanits, "You see that I have created many other gods. I have appointed you to be their ruler. You will initiate the other gods." And she gave him blades of yucca plant with which to perform this initiation.

Then Iatiku took more dirt from the basket and gave life to Kopishtai'ya and his wife. [39]Iatiku said, "You look ferocious so you will have to live in a different place."

Then Iatiku turned to Tsitsanits and told him, "You are going to be chief of the katsina and will rule over them. Take them with you to Wenimats, [40]west and south of here. [This place was described as a place where there was a lake with weeds growing in it and under this lake is Wenimats.] There is where you are going to live. Bring happiness to my people. Whenever my people want you they will send you hachamoni [41] (prayer sticks)." So Iatiku made one so Tsitsanits would know it, and made one for each kind of katsina so each would know his own prayer stick. When they [the prayer sticks] were sent they [the katsina] would have to answer.

After giving all the prayer sticks, Iatiku told Tsitsanits to make a song of their own which must be very pretty so as to give happiness to her people. So this is the way Iatiku sent them to Wenimats and told them to wait for their prayer sticks from her people and to be always prepared to come. "Your people and my people will be combined," she said. "You will give us food from your world and we will give you food from our world. Your people are to represent clouds; you are to bring rain, you are to rule the summer clouds." Iatiku told them to take along animals as they would also be permitted to be hunters. Iatiku then took up the basket of corn meal, pollen, tobacco, and prayer sticks, and made the road open for them four lengths (long distance) to Wenimats and return by which they could come back when needed. Then she gave Tsitsanits the basket.

Kopishtaiya remained, and Iatiku turned to him saying, "You are to be separate from the others." He was given the same sort of instructions and prayer sticks and told to go east to Hakuoi'kŭchahǎ, [42] to the place where the sun rises. "You are going to represent, and rule the winter clouds. My people will pray to you to obtain bravery and long, healthy life. In the winter time my people will send you prayer sticks." Thus she spoke.

After Iatiku had instructed Kopishtaiya she gave him the basket with pollen, corn meal, tobacco, and prayer sticks. She made the road four lengths to the east and return, and told them to make their home at Hakuoikuchaha. So this is the way Iatiku placed the rulers of the clouds to whom her people were to pray.

After this was done Iatiku was thinking of leaving, so she told her people, "Now you are going to make homes here." So when she spoke the words, "nano ūs'thē i'chĭn," [43] there grew up all of a sudden a house. Iatiku told her people, "This is the kind of a house you are going to build to live in." So her people started to build one of their own, using this as a model. Iatiku gathered some rocks and dirt for them and sticks. All of them grew and multiplied till ready for use. So they made a town. Iatiku laid out the plans for the town and laid out the plaza. After this was done, she started to instruct her people. She called the first man who was born in the Antelope clan and said to him, "You are to be Tiamuni [44] and the father of the katsina. [45] You are the one to welcome them when they come." So, Iatiku made him a ya'paishĭ'ni [46] (altar), the first one to be made. So Iatiku said, "Let us try and see if everything works all right. We will call the katsina." So she taught the people how to maker prayer sticks and taught them the prayers. It took 4 days to make these up. They were instructed to bring all their prayer sticks to the altar of the Antelope clan (pl. 3, fig. 1) and place them in a basket. They had four baskets full. So all of the Antelope clan took these baskets and offered them to the katsina and asked them to come. They took them to the west and buried them. In praying they make four motions so as to cover the four lengths of the road. After this was done, the prayer sticks all went to the katsina. Then Tsitsanits took them and told each one of the katsina they were called to visit the people at Shipapu (where they still were). So the katsina prayed to the clouds with these same prayer sticks, and they smoked the cigarettes that were in the baskets so that clouds would come into them. Tsitsanits told Gomaiowish to go back to Iatiku's people and tell them that they [the katsina] were coming on the fourth day. "We are going to bring them provisions and corn," he said. So the Goniaiowish went.

When he got to Shipapu, the Antelope chief met him and he received the message. [47]Gomaiowish left and Antelope chief told all the people the message that he had received and said that everyone was to expect the katsina on the fourth day. So Iatiku told her people, "Let us also prepare to welcome them with our food." So she called for a tribal hunt. Everyone who killed anything prepared it in his own home the day they expected the katsina to come. So it really happened that they came that day. They came in a cloud and everything (food, etc.) was brought. Gomaiowish was in the lead and told of their approach.

When they arrived they were met by the Antelope clan chief. [48]So the chief pointed out to them the different places they were to dance on the plaza: First on the north side, then west, then south, then east side. After the katsina finished the four dances they were brought inside where the altar was to rest. At this time there were no kivas; they were just trying out. The people were much interested in the katsina and were very happy over the visit. The katsina had their own songs. So the people were instructed to take food to the house where they were but they were not allowed to enter the room, only members of the Antelope clan, who served them were allowed to enter. This was at noon. In the afternoon, after each dance, the katsina gave the people presents of the food they had brought. Among the presents given out were throwing-sticks (bow and arrows had not been made yet), clothing of the katsina (not masks). Before the katsina left, Gomaiowish announced that the katsina did not wish to leave them entirely find told them to take their presents and use them for any dance that they wanted to put on, in the town (for happiness). So before they left they stripped, all except their masks, and gave the people their clothing as presents. (The Acoma still do this when they finish dancing; as a rule they distribute their costumes to their near relatives.)

So the Antelope chief bade the katsina goodbye and they left. Iatiku said, "So far all is well but there are some things needed yet. We have no sacred place, we have no kaach [49](kiva)." Iatiku said, "this is the way I emerged, so I guess we will make a house in the ground, which we will call kaach. This will be the sacred place for the katsina when they come." (The kivas were round at first, now they are square. At the foot of the mesa where the old town was all washed away the kiva was round.)

When they began to build the first kiva, Iatiku told Oak man that it must be done in a certain way. Then she told him just how it was to be done. The whole kiva was to represent Shipapu, the place of emergence, though in ceremonial language it is called mauharo kai [50]

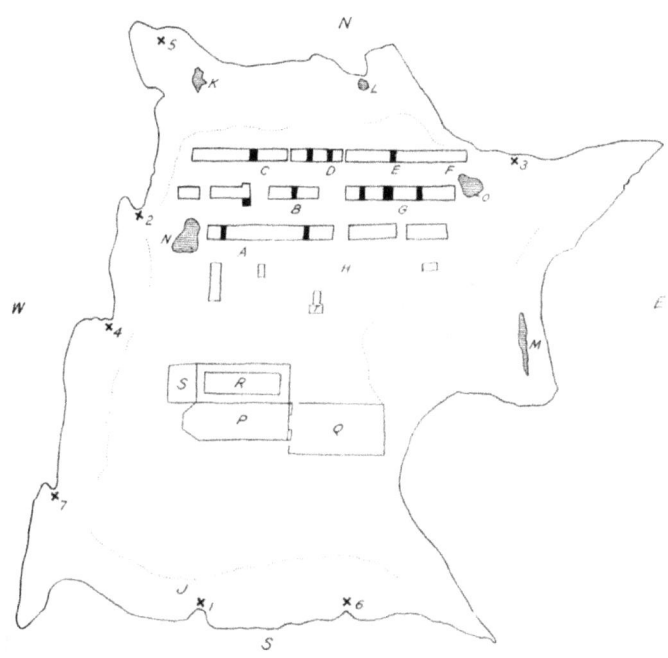

FIGURE 1.--Plan of Acoma

1, Rainbow (Kastiatsi) trail, by which the people first entered Acoma. 2, Ladder trail. 3, Cliff trail (very steep). 4, Sand trail. 5, Crack trail (not used always). 6, Ladder crack trail. 7, Burro trail. Black line, high cliff; dotted line, edge of mesa, second cliff (low). A-H, Places where katsina dance. J, Place where dancers dress. K, L, M. Cisterns for drinking water. N, O, Cisterns for washing, plastering, etc. Houses have rock foundation and the first floor is of rock. From there up. adobe. P, Church. Q, Cemetery. R, Convento. S, Corral where burros were kept. T, Komaxira meeting house built by Spaniards (the dark underworld where the Sisters were found; Shipapu is the upper part of the place of emergence where there was some light).[51]

When they built the kiva, they first put up beams of four different trees. These were the trees that were planted in the underworld for the people to climb up on. In the north, under the foundation they placed yellow turquoise; in the west, blue turquoise; in the south, red, and in the east, white turquoise. Prayer sticks are placed at each place so the foundation will be strong and will never give way. The walls represent the sky, the beams of the roof (made of wood of the first four trees) represent the Milky Way, wakaiyanistiawï'tsa (way-above-earth beam). The sky looks like a circle, hence the round shape of the kiva.

The medicine man was instructed to make a fireplace inside the kiva. This fireplace is right under the ladder and is called kohaiya (bear) (fig. 2, A). In front of the fireplace is tsiwaimitiima (another-altar-placed-under). It is a hollow place in the floor in which an altar like the one Iatiku first made is kept. It is covered with a board (fig. 2, B). The chianyi are the only ones who are allowed to dance on it. It gives out a hollow sound. [52]Iatiku said that whenever a medicine man wanted to get more superhuman power for himself he was to dance and roll over this altar.

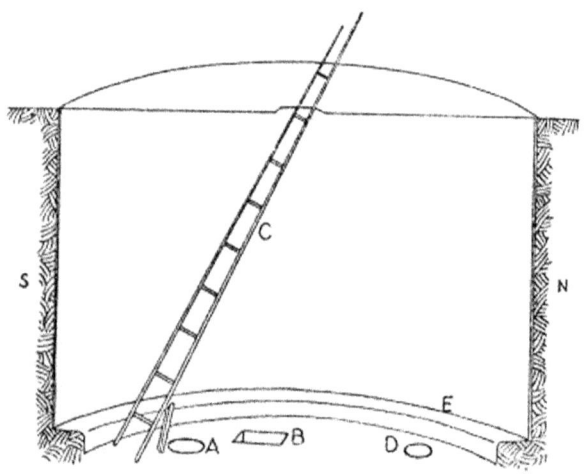

FIGURE 2.--Diagram of kiva, showing fog seats.

The ladder (fig. 2, C) represents the rainbow (kastiatsi).

On the north is a hollow dug-out place that represents the door of North Mountain, East Mountain, West Mountain, Sun and Moon (fig. 2, D). Whenever they pray to these powers (kūa'watsaiishu'mă, "powers that rule") they pray into this doorway.

Around the entire base of the kiva are he'ăshită'nămă (fog seats) (fig. 2, E), imaginary seats of fog covered with bear skins or lion skins. (All this is described in prayer.) Spirits are invited in prayer to come and sit on these seats. Actually, only fetishes are in the kiva; the real spirits are out in the mountains of the cardinal points. They are invited to come and to be present during ceremonies, and they are supposed to be seated there.

Iatiku ordered that people should always enter the kiva facing the ladder as soon as a foot is placed on it. When entering or leaving the kiva, one should never turn back after starting. This is because when Nautsiti and Iatiku came up from the lower world they went on up without turning back or without stopping. If anyone turns back, it will shorten his life; he will leave his soul in the kiva. If someone should do this, his relatives will have to buy back his life by bringing food to the kiva. When they go to the top of the ladder with the food, they call down inside, "Chima!" (Below!)

The ladder must be made of wood of the four first trees of the underworld. Nautsiti and Iatiku did not know where the pine trees touched, and they do not know where the rainbow touches, so they call the ladder "Rainbow."

When you get down to the foot of the ladder in the kiva, you must always go to the right and take a seat; never to the left. When you leave, you must circle round to the right. Never take fire from the front of the fireplace, nor step into it. Never whistle in the kiva. All these were the rules that Iatiku laid down for the conduct of the kiva.

Iatiku said, "I think someone ought to be the father of the game animals-- shay·'ik [53] will be his name. His work will be the power of his songs. When he sings and prays to the animals they (hunters) will be partners to the prey animals." She picked the oldest man born in the Eagle clan because the eagle is a bird of prey. His work was to sing the songs with the people when they go out to hunt because he was the only one to know the prayers belonging to the prey animals. So Iatiku taught him songs and prayers and gave him an altar (pl. 8, fig. 1) with which to secure the power of the animals that kill, to come and be in his people. So Iatiku said, "Let us try it out and see if it will work out right." So this chosen man set up his altar and Iatiku taught him to make prayer sticks to give to the man who was going on a hunt and taught him to make fetishes representing the beasts of prey. So Eagle. Man called a meeting at his house where the altar was, so they could sing the songs that had been taught him. They sang these songs all night. Early in the morning, Eagle Man gave prayer sticks to each man who had been singing and told him to go out and pray in the wilds. They were called shaiyai'kă (hunter's Society): They prayed so that they would have the power of the prey animals. So the chief of the hunters' society (the Eagle Man),started out early the fourth morning to a place he had selected. On his way whenever he saw tracks of animals, even small ones, he would take some dirt out of the track, and dung, and place it in a cedar bark container like a dish. When he came to the designated place he tied both ends of the cedar bark with yucca blades. He was going to scorch the feet of the game animals. [54]Then he made a fire and scorched the dirt and dung so as to scorch the feet of the animals so they could not run fast. (This fire is made in a natural way with a fire drill.)

After this to give the signal for the people to come he threw green branches on the fire to make a smoke. Eagle Man had already told the men that when they went out to meet at the camp they were to bring along sacred corn meal and pollen and also to pick up any dung or dirt from animals' tracks they passed; so when they came to the fire they were to throw it in, to help scorch their feet. When they threw it on the fire they were to name any animal they wished to help them on the hunt, birds for small game like rabbits; lion, wolf, wildcat, for deer and large game. So everyone upon coming to the camp did this. Usually a high spot was picked as meeting place, so they could watch and not start the hunt if someone was still on his way to the meeting place. When all were in camp, the Eagle Man told the people, "Now we are going north, west, south or east on a drive, stirring up the game in the brush." He advised the men that when they go on a hunt, that when they stop they should pray with corn meal to Mother Earth, so they would not be injured, or blamed for killing the animals. Then he selected two men from his clan who were to lead two lines of men in a wide circle. These lines were to meet at a place designated by Eagle Man. They were instructed to carry some fire with them (torches of cedar bark), so that they could signal when the two lines met.

They were also instructed to observe several rules: When you throw a stick and hit a game animal, if it does not get up, it's yours. If two sticks hit about the same time and kill it, the one who says, "shi" (mine) first gets it. If you hit a rabbit and knock it down, but it gets up and is killed by another, the one who stops it gets it.--This was to avoid any argument on the hunt for small game.

RULE FOR TRACKING LARGE GAME

SUPPOSE a man starts early in the morning tracking an animal. Another man starts later and comes in ahead and kills the animal. It belongs to the one who first started to track it.

After hunting all day, when the people were about to make the last circle, Eagle Man announced that if anyone killed anything in this last circle it would belong to him (the killer). All the other game was to go to the Antelope Man for food for the katsina. (The reason Iatiku had made Antelope Man leader (chief) was so when the katsina came he would have food brought to him to feed the katsina.)[55] Eagle Man then announced, "You may go home and rest."

The day after the hunt, the people who had killed game were supposed to roast it and have it ready for the Eagle Man, who was to gather it up and bring it to the Antelope Man. This was the instruction given by Eagle Man at the last announcement on the hunt: "If a rabbit, you are to skin it carefully and save the skin. Break the upper part of the legs of the rabbit and fold the front legs across the breast and hind legs across the back." He told them to take some, corn meal and pollen and place them under each leg of the rabbit, to thank Mother Earth and pray that she would raise more game. He also told them not to put the rabbit into the fire or coals head first when roasting it, but to face it out so its spirit could escape and return to be reborn and thus furnish more game. The spirit of the rabbit would take with it as food the corn and pollen offerings placed under the legs.

Such were the instructions to the hunters. They were always to be followed so they would have game.

When a deer is killed, it is cut up where it falls; the legs are cut off and the ribs taken out. The head, the backbone, and the skin are all connected in one piece. When cut open, the entrails are placed to one side on the ground. The bladder is taken out and placed in the center of the entrails [56] and the hunter prays that the deer be reborn and that he will have good luck with game. He has corn meal and pollen and pieces of beads and shells which he sprinkles on.--All of these practices are according to instructions given by Eagle Man on the first hunt.

FETISHES

WHEN hunters go on a big hunt they get fetishes from Eagle Man which they bring along. When the hunter takes the heart out, the fetish is made to drink blood from the heart. These fetishes are kept in each family, Iatiku made the first one for Eagle Man and he taught the others how to make them. They should be made of a hard stone, flint, or gypsum, with eyes of turquoise set in pitch. Small ones are carried for protection and because they represent the prey animals. Any man can make a fetish, which he may call wolf, lion, or whatever he pleases. He then brings it to the Eagle Man of the Hunters' society. The Eagle Man and the society then pray to it and sing over it, putting into it the spirit and the power of the lion (north), wolf (west), lynx (south), wildcat (east). The power of the fetish is drawn from all these equally.

The head man holds the fetish in the palms of his hands, swinging it to the four directions to the following song:

It comes alive
It comes alive, alive, alive.
In the north mountain
The lion comes alive
In the north mountain, comes alive.
With this the prey animal
Will have power to attract deer, antelope;
Will have power to be lucky.

(Repeat for wolf of the west, lynx of the south, and wildcat of the east.) With each verse the Eagle Man faces the direction indicated, swinging his hands in that direction. The man who holds the fetish (head man) is praying another way and does not sing with the other singers. When the song is finished the fetish is laid in front of the altar beside the fetishes of the society where it remains over night. During this time it becomes alive. The next day it is given to its owner. When the new fetish has been placed in front of the altar each member of the society in turn approaches it and says, "Drink the blood of the lion (or whatever it has been named)."

In the kiva is one large, fetish representing each of the four beasts of prey: múkaiïtchă, "lion" (n); kakan, "wolf" (w); shohóna,[57]"lynx" (s); gyat "wildcat" (e). These names are preceded by Shaiyaika (Hunters' society) to indicate that they are fetishes. Each fetish is placed in its proper direction in front of the altar. The fetish to be given life is placed alongside the one for which it is named. The head man, when he places it in front of the altar, places it by its "mother" from which it draws its power, and it leaves as offspring of quoting from S. F. Baird, Mammals of the Mexican Boundary, 1857, pp. 7-8. See, also, Bailey, 1937, pp. 283-284). Coronado's letter to Mendoza of August 3, 1540, sneaks of lions and tigers [jaguars] (Winship, 1896, p. 560).} the "mother." When the fetish is returned, it still has a connection with the one on the altar. It may be recalled from the owner if the society wants to use it. This is often done when the owner has been lucky in the hunt. When the society finishes with it, it is returned to the owner. These fetishes are handed down in the family.[58]

When a hunter kills an antelope or a deer he brings it into the pueblo. The father or mother of the [hunter's] house comes out with some corn meal in her hand with which she makes a "road" into the house and up the ladder, if they live above. Then they help the hunter with his pack, and lay the deer on the floor with its head toward the fireplace, about 10 feet from the fire. Beads are laid on the neck. (Beads of lignite are preferred, as the hoofs of the deer are supposed to be made of this substance.) The deer would wear these back. They are taken away when they think the spirit has left, in about an hour. If relatives of the hunter come in, they go up to the deer and touch it and then rub their hands over their faces because they say the deer is pretty and not lazy. They say, "We are glad you have come to our home and have not been ashamed of our people." A dish of corn meal is placed near by and all visitors feed a little to the deer asking him to come next to their house, as they believe the deer will be reborn.

When the beads are taken off, they blow them into the other room. (Beads are supposed to have power to attract; women wear beads to attract men.) They then start to skin the animal up to the neck. The skin is all taken off. The head is boiled in a pot without taking the horns off. In the pot is placed corn, pumpkin seeds, and piñon nuts. These are called the deer's ear rings. Before they eat this the hunter would call the clan of his father (not mother) to come and help eat the head. The mother of the hunter's father, if still living, takes the eyes and eats them. If she is not there, the oldest female relative in the father's clan does this. The hunter, or any man, is supposed not to eat the eyes of a deer lest he always have water in his eyes (tears) and not be able to see far. The hunter must not eat the tongue as this will make him thirsty. Nor may he eat the udder lest his teeth not be strong.

After the meat is all eaten from the head, it will be placed on top of the house to dry. When he has time, the hunter takes it back into the mountains where he prays that it will come alive again. First it must be painted as the deer was originally. A black line is painted down the middle of the face; under the jaw is white. Balls of cotton are stuffed in the eye sockets and the centers painted black. Then a string is tied across the antlers and to this feathers are attached.[59]

All large game is treated like the deer: mountain sheep, elk, buffalo, also lions, lynx, bear. Rabbit skulls are treated in the same way except that they are not painted or prepared in any way.

This is the way Iatiku made the first hunting society.

WANDERINGS, PART I

THE game was all gathered and saved for the katsina at the house of Antelope clan. After this had been done, the men who had been taught the hunting songs, made songs of their own, rejoicing over the hunt, and put on a dance in honor of the Eagle Man and proclaimed him leader of the hunt. Then Iatiku said, "Let us try again to call the katsina." So she asked the Antelope Man to call the katsina again. Antelope Man notified the people to pray for the katsina to visit them again and for them to bring their prayer sticks to his altar. Antelope Man took the baskets of prayer sticks, prayed, and buried them in the ground. They were received at Wenimats.

So it happened again as before. The messenger Gomaiowish was again sent out to notify the people that the katsina were coming on the fourth day. So four women from the Antelope clan were selected to prepare the food that had been brought in by the Eagle Man for a feast. And every household was asked to bring some flour to the Antelope clan altar. The four women also prepared this for the katsina. The other time, Iatiku saw that the people had to bring food to the door where the katsina were staying. This was why she called the community hunt so the people would not have to come around again. Now only the Antelope clan were permitted to serve the katsina. So everything happened all right. They were taken care of at the Antelope elan altar and Iatiku said, "All is well. Now it does not seem to me that we are playing with the katsina; they are now to be regarded as sacred." (The first visit had been rather informal; the katsina were treated much as human visitors.)

Iatiku was satisfied that everything worked well with the katsina part. But she saw that the Antelope clan was carrying too much of the burden, so she thought of making another officer to be called tsa'tia hochani, [60] the war chief. She selected the first man in the Sky clan, because he was to rule on the outside. He was to be above the Eagle Man, that is, to rank above him and above all other officers. Whatever he says goes. In the old days this office was always from the Sky clan. [61] Iatiku called this man and said, "I am going to make you tsa'tia hochani." So she made for him what is called hachamoni kaiok [62] (broken prayer stick) (pl. 5, fig. 2). It has the four trails marked on the four sides. This would extend from the earth up to the sky. [63] She gave it to him and told him, "When you hold it clasped in your hands, you are drawing all the people together so they will not be scattered. With this you will have great power over all the rest of the people. You will have them tucked under your arms, [64] and their minds will be tucked in your temples" (meaning "you will do their thinking for them and speak for them; you will be their mind"). Then Iatiku taught him his prayers. His prayers should always start from Shipapu. After coming up from Shipapu, they should start from the north and take in the west, south, and east. This is a very long prayer.

He was told that he would rule [officiate] around these places but he was not to be paid for his services; [65] he would represent the people and pray for them. (This is still done.)

Before this the Antelope clan was ruling everything. The Country Chief took the burden of all rule outside the pueblo. Iatiku told him. that he was to have the hardest work, that he was the one to go out and meet the katsina and bring the message to the Antelope clan, and that it was his duty to notify the people by crying out all matters of importance relating to outside.

Now Iatiku said, "Let's try to call the katsina." (They were still at Shipapu.) All was done as before and when all was over Iatiku said things worked out better. But she saw that Country Chief was carrying too much of the burden so she thought of giving him two helpers. She selected the first two sons (or maybe brothers) of Country Chief. She called the oldest one who was to be next in rank Shuti mut (wren youth). [66] The other was to be called Shpa'ti mut (mocking bird youth). [67] In this order they were to rank. Iatiku named them thus because they were to represent these birds, to make their sounds, and to bring messages to the people, thus relieving Country Chief. (It is very different now. Today they call them the two cooks because they serve the head man. They prepare his corn meal and pollen so he will always have plenty. Now they have Spanish names.)

Country Chief had to go out and pray every fourth day to the north, another 4 days to the west, another 4 days to the South, and 4 more days to the east. (Now they take turns, and the three of them do it, making the burden easier. These helpers also help as town criers.) Everything was tried out again and Iatiku was satisfied.

Country Chief was also instructed to watch the seasons. He was to go out in the country each day to watch the plants. At this time the only way they could tell the seasons was by the growth of the plants. Country Chief was to tell the people what season they were ending or approaching. (It is told in later tradition that Country Chief started to watch the stars and moon and, being able to tell seasons more accurately in this way, he abandoned the method of watching the plants. Country Chief also watched the sun to determine the time for the solstices. Now the Antelope chief does this.) [68] (Sun is male, Moon female; hence men are strong, women weaker.) The katsina that live in the east come for the winter solstice and the katsina that live in the west come for the summer solstice. [69]

They lived for a long time with these officers. Finally, when everything seemed all right with the katsina of the west, Iatiku decided to try the katsina of the east. (These are not called katsina but Kopishtaiya. The first was Tsiukiri (pl. 4, fig. 2) who went with his mate and reproduced. His mate is Hi'waii'tsa.) [70] So Iatiku told Country Chief to tell the Antelope Man that they were going to try and call the Kopishtaiya (pl. 6, fig. 2), who live where the sun comes up, and to make preparations. So the Antelope Man said, "It is all right. Go and tell the people to wait for them and prepare for them by gathering material to make prayer sticks."

So Country Chief told his two helpers to go out and before cutting sticks for prayer sticks they should say the prayer, "Come and help us, Yellow Flint! Come, Red Flint, come White Flint! Help us! You are the ones who are really going to cut the prayer sticks." Thus he taught them the song they were to sing when they started to cut the prayer sticks with the flints. These that they brought in were to be used at the broken prayer stick of Country Chief. So Country Chief came out to meet them as they brought in the sticks. (They would stop outside and cry gaiya' (inside), so as not to interrupt any ceremony that might be going on. Nowadays they knock on the door.) So Country Chief made a trail for them to come inside and they brought their sticks in. They were instructed to bring them on the fourth day.

On the fourth day all the prayer sticks were brought in. They made a prayer stick that was to look like the ones given to the kopishtaiya by Iatiku so they would recognize them. So the prayer sticks were brought in and Antelope Man went out to the east with them in baskets, prayed, and buried them. Four days from that time, he said, the people were to wait for the Kopishtaiya. They had no messenger like the messenger of the katsina, but the people were sure they would come. Just before sun-up Country Chief heard them singing in the east, so he sent messages in the village that the Kopishtaiya were coming near. The Kopishtaiya were not dancers, they came only to circle the outside of the village. At intervals they went around the village, prayed, and put up dapi'nǎshtimĭt, [71] spiritual fortifications or protections. After circling the town they came into the plaza. The people saw that they had seeds in bags with them. They were all naked save for breech clouts made of rabbit skins. They wore no moccasins even though it was very cold, for they represented strong, hardy men. They gave presents of seed to the people and told them to plant these seeds. After they had finished distributing them they left. They thanked the people for praying with prayer sticks and food (as is daily custom) and then they left. Iatiku saw that they were real and that all went well so she told the people to believe in them also.

Some time after this the evil spirit (Pishuni) came to the people of Iatiku in the form of disease. It had by this time grown of itself into a big power, and the people were stricken with a plague. It is not known what form of disease it was for the people had never known sickness before. They were panic stricken. They tried by every way, gathering plants and making drinks, to relieve themselves but nothing helped them. So Iatiku thought of choosing a man to be known as chaianyi (medicine man). So she called Country Chief and told him what she was thinking of doing. Country Chief said, "All right." So Iatiku told him, "I have told you to watch your people and to know them, so I will leave it up to you to select the man." Iatiku wished the Antelope clan man and the Eagle man to be present at a council together with the three Country Chiefs. The meeting was held. Country Chief stood up and told the others that he would select the first man from the Oak clan to be first chaianyi, and his altar would be named hakan chaianyi (fire medicine man). He chose this man because he represented a strong wood for making fire, and he called it [the altar] fire medicine man because it was one of the first strong things given to Iatiku. (Fire was one of the most powerful forces and oak was the best wood for it.) So everyone in the council agreed upon the one who was chosen, so Country Chief gave the name of the altar to Iatiku, and said, "This is the man we have chosen."

WANDERINGS, PART II

EVERYBODY was still living, no one had died yet. So the oldest man of the Oak clan was notified that he had been chosen and that he was to come to the broken prayer stick. So they brought him in and told him he had been chosen as the man to be helpful when any sickness came among the people. "You will be the means of their recovery." Then they told him that Iatiku was going to instruct him and care for him, (i. e., would give him his altar and paraphernalia). So Iatiku told him to come to her and she then told him to go to North Mountain to look for a pine tree that had been struck by lightning, and to take some of the split wood from the blasted part. "You will also find hati [72] (obsidian) which also will be used by you." She told him to bring all this back to her. Then she taught him how to make the black prayer stick as a symbol of the dark, for he was instructed to work at night. She told him to make four of these and to carry them with him when he went to seek the pine and obsidian. "You will also find there an arrowhead with which the pine was struck down." (Even today at Acoma they think there is an arrowhead where lightning has struck. These are sought and worn as amulets.) With this he would have protection; it would be his heart or soul.

So the Oak Man took these four prayer sticks to the north and there he prayed with them and buried them. Then he looked for the pine tree and finally found everything as predicted by Iatiku. He gathered some of the flat split wood into a bundle. He also found some obsidian and the arrowhead. These he brought back. His relatives and clan knew why he had been away and were waiting for him when he returned. The Oak Man told Iatiku that he had brought the things he had been instructed to get. Iatiku told him that he was to make an altar for himself and he was to use the obsidian for a knife. Iatiku taught him to make the altar and the altar prayer sticks (pl. 9, fig. 2). He finished the altar which is commonly called Iatiku (pl. 8, fig. 2). Then Iatiku told Oak Man to make a sand painting (pl. 10, fig. 2). The painting will be blue and circular to represent the sky. The earth is hanging from the Milky Way. This is because the Milky Way is like a beam holding up the earth. This is because the Milky Way does not change its position but is always circling in the east. The head of the earth faces east; the feet are in the west, with arms outstretched north and south. Thus, as the earth lies facing upward, the sun rises over its head and passes over its body lengthwise, setting at its feet. In the ceremony the medicine bowl is always set on the heart with a special prayer. Thus the Medicine derives its strength from the heart of the earth. Sun, Moon, and Stars are drawn as alive with eyes and mouth (pl. 11). (Sun, Moon, Stars are the most powerful of forces. Sun gives everything strength. It gives the seeds in the earth strength to sprout, and this strength is imparted to us when we eat these plants.)

Then Iatiku taught him the songs and showed him how to make two fetishes which were to represent the bear. [73] He was going to have the power of the bear, so Iatiku spoke to the bear and said, "You will be a partner to this chaianyi." And Iatiku also spoke to the eagle and told him he was to be a partner of the chaianyi. The bear was to represent the power of all the animals that live on earth, and the eagle the power of all the birds that fly in the air. Iatiku also spoke to mayatup [74] (weasel) to be partner with the chaianyi and to represent all the animals that live within the ground. The next thing Iatiku made for him was a square bowl called waitichani, the medicine bowl which Iatiku instructed Oak Man's wife to make from mitsa (a fine clay). So she made the bowl and Iatiku told her to make drawings of two bears on the front; on the back, a picture of an eagle; and on the bottom, the weasel. (Nowadays they put on lizard, Snakes, and clouds besides.) This was the origin of pottery. This particular pot was for mixing medicine. Iatiku told Oak Man then to got branches of the spruce (hakak) and fir (gaiaits'ti'up ? piñon) and the roots of tschuma (an aromatic herb; the roots taste sweet) and another root. He was instructed to grind the four plants together and to have some prepared. Iatiku also told him to get the left front paw of a bear and to skin it a little above the wrist with the claws still on it, and to take all the claws of the other three feet and make a necklace of them, and to place the skin back of the altar. [75] She said, "Get the left front paw because that is the bear's best hand. Boars are quicker on the left." The two bear fetishes were to be painted with the bear's blood. On the altar were also two eagle and two weasel fetishes.

Iatiku told Oak Man he was to kill an eagle and take the longest feather from each wing [76] and the down from under the tail, and to tie them on the top of the last two uprights of the altar. [77] He was also to bring all the rest of the feathers. Iatiku then told him to kill a weasel, to place the skin as the foundation (carpet) for the altar, and to place the two front paws with the fetish. The paws look like human hands and the weasel uses them like hands. Blood from the heart of the eagle was used to paint the eagle fetishes, and weasel blood was smeared on the weasel fetishes.

Iatiku then told him to kill a mallard duck (teal), skin it and take the green feathers from the wings and bring them to the altar. Iatiku told him to get an abalone shell and in the west mountain to get turquoise. He was to make a string of beads from the turquoise and abalone shell. Iatiku told him this would be something sacred and instructed him how to make the beads. She told him not to throw away the chips broken off but to save them, because "these chips will also be sacred and you will use them to pray with." [78] Now all was finished but one thing. "You are to make a drum and a rattle. The drum (pl. 12, fig. 1) you are to make from ha'ati (a tree that grows a layer each year). Knock the center out and use the outside cylinder. Cover both ends with the skin of the elk." She instructed him how to lace the skin on. Then she taught him how to make the drumstick out of wood of the same tree. When the drum was finished he was taught how to make the rattle. "Take the scrotum of the elk; take the hair off and stuff it with dry sand and let it dry, tying a stick in it first. When it is dry, pour the sand out. Then put some agave seeds into the rattle." [79] Thus it was finished.

At this time Iatiku lived alone in a house on an island in a lake. She lived alone on this island and the people lived all around the lake. She was visited only by Country Chief. While getting instructions for the altar, he ran back and forth to the island. Country Chief would pass the instructions on to Oak Man. Now Iatiku said, "It is my turn. I will make for you honani." [80] She instructed Oak Man to bring her the feathers of the eagle and duck that were not used on the altar, the tail feathers of shaask (roadrunner), and the tail feathers of magpie, and to bring some cotton and the ear of corn called tsatchikotsch. [81] This is an ear which has the kernels clear up to the top with no open space at top of cob. It is very rare. After they had brought these things to Iatiku she called Country Chief and his two helpers and told them to guard around her house, that her place was going to be secret, and no one was to bother her. The trail that led to Iatiku's house was paved with abalone shell. Abalone shells came from this lake.

So Iatiku made this honani with corn in the center into which she had blown her own breath, into the hollow in the bottom of the cob, and then closed it with the cotton. This breath was to be her own power in it; she blew her heart (soul) into it. This ear of corn would thereafter symbolize herself, as she was thinking of leaving the people. [82] She then covered it with four layers of corn husk. After she blew her breath into the hollow of the ear, she put some honey into the hollow before she closed it up with cotton. This was food for her breath and would be food for all time for the people. Honey was chosen because it comes from all kinds of plants and it therefore symbolizes all plant food. This honey in the cob meant that there would always be food. It would be as a seed or source of all food to come. The Oak Man was present while the honani was being made and he was instructed how it was made, so that when it became necessary to make another it would be up to him. When a man is made a medicine man is the only time a new honani is made. Today there are many of these honani which carry the power of Iatiku. They are kept in the family always. If a medicine society wants one they borrow it from some family.

After wrapping the corn ear in four husks, Iatiku took the skin of the duck's head and a turquoise and placed them under the corn as a seat. Over the top and around the outside husks she spread cotton. The duck skin with blue feathers was placed under the turquoise because the color was like turquoise. From now on the turquoise was going to have a lot of power, the power to make one attractive and to be loved. The breath Iatiku blew into the cob would be all powerful as far as the air extended, but no farther. [83] The roadrunner and magpie and eagle down and turkey feathers (the short tail feathers--there were no parrots then), and the down from under the tail of the eagle were used, (Nowadays just "pretty" feathers are used.) These feathers from then on were to be useful in making prayers. The green wing feathers of the duck were placed in front hiding the face. Then the string of abalone, turquoise, and shell beads was placed above the honani. All these things were to be sacred and valuable from then on. All things that went into the making of the honani were to be regarded as sacred. The whole thing would represent Iatiku.

After Iatiku had taught Oak Man all this she taught the making of the yapaishe altar. It took a long time to teach Oak Man the prayers and songs. After he had learned everything, Iatiku said, "Let us try it out. You are to work 4 days and these 4 days you are not to touch a woman. You are going to eat special food during this time: beans without salt, corn, wa'ak, [84] muni (plant), i'mǎ'ǎshchǎ. None of this food can be mixed with meat." The fourth night was to be the night he would work.

WANDERINGS, PART III

IATIKU had three more things in her basket. She knew that there were two eggs, parrot, and crow, but the third thing she did not know, so she decided to bring it to life, and see what it was. So she said, "Come alive! Let us see what you are like." And at her words it came alive. It said, "Why have I come alive? Am I wanted?" Iatiku said, "Do not ask. You will be useful." It came to life in the form of a human (male). Koshari was kind of crazy; he was active, picking around, talking nonsense, talking backward, etc. Iatiku did not think much of him, so she sent him to the Oak Man to see if he would be of any use there. So Koshari went, saying, "I know everything. Sure I'll go and I'll do everything for him, I'll be a big help." (This he said though he was just born and had no experience.)

Koshari rushed to the pueblo, climbing the wall to get in, asking every one where the altar of the Oak Man was. He spoke very loudly around the altar, even though it was supposed to be very quiet there. After he had finally bumped into Country Chief, who was guarding the altar, Koshari asked, "Where is this mauharo kai'ye (kiva of the medicine man)?" He tried to go in directly, so Country Chief caught him. "But," he protested, "I have been sent here. I am allowed everywhere by Iatiku." So Country Chief let him go, saying, "Well, he may be of some use." So Koshari yelled into the kiva, "I'm coming down," and without awaiting response or permission, he went down. As soon as he reached the bottom he said, "I came here as your partner. I have been sent to help you. I can do anything." The Oak Man was glad to have someone help him. But Koshari waited for nothing but went right to work and placed the different objects in front of the altar, saying, "Let me do it! I can do it." So Oak Man did not keep him from doing anything. He caused Oak Man a lot of amusement, in his heretofore solitary life, with his garbled speech and wisecracking and his self-confidence. (Before Iatiku told him [Koshari] to go to the altar, she told him, "I am going to initiate you. I am going to be there myself.")

All this happened on the fourth day of Oak Man's fast. Iatiku had instructed Oak Man to have a fire built in front of the altar and some yellow corn prepared. Iatiku also instructed Country Chief to tell the people to be quiet and wait during these 4 days as Iatiku was going to bring the honani to life. Country Chief told the people that the chaianyi was going to fast these 4 days and that the people should cook food for him on the fourth day. So as soon as it grew dark, Koshari spoke up, saying, "It is time now, let me go after Iatiku." So he went after her and brought her. So Iatiku, when she came to the kiva roof, called, "Chima!" Koshari, who had rushed in ahead, said, "Come on in, it is all right with us." So Iatiku, when she had come in, Said, "koa'tsi kanai skauchani daimi, [85] (Greetings, mother, my officers [chiefs].) Now you are passing this far in the day. From now on it will be by you that the pueblo will be run." So Koshari and the Oak Man said, "All right, but it is from you." So Koshari took Iatiku by the hand and set her down behind the altar. Iatiku asked the Oak Man if Koshari was of any use. Oak Man replied, "Yes, he has been very useful." Koshari agreed, "Yes, I know it, I am an expert at all this." So Oak Man asked Iatiku if all was all right, if the altar and everything suitably represented her. Iatiku said, "Yes, I am going to give myself to represent this altar and honani. It will also represent long life, luck, harvest, and game. The altar will have power over all of these." So Iatiku asked Oak Man to pass her "my sister," the honani.

They started to sing the song that was to establish the altar and give it life, in fact to represent her. Koshari sang the loudest and kept a line or so ahead of the rest. After this song was finished, Iatiku told Oak Man to tell the people that wished to come in to bring food for the altar and the medicine man. So Koshari got up saying, "Let me go up and tell Country Chief." So Koshari told Country Chief that he was all ready for them. "I'm all ready to eat, bring the food!" So the people (i. e., certain families who had been selected by Country Chief) brought the food.

It was dark now, so Iatiku told Oak Man to offer the food to the "ones that are ahead of you," i. e., to the now living altar. So the medicine man placed the food in front of the altar and started to pray, gesturing the food toward the spirits or the altar. In the song-prayer, Oak Man asks help, saying, "I am just a common man. I am not superhuman. My hands have no skill" [86] Koshari was doing the same thing. Iatiku told Oak Man to have some of the food. "When you finish, you are to offer it to the earth the next day, thus giving it back." After a few minutes, Iatiku spoke to Oak Man, saying, "Now that you have set this offering aside, you may break your fast on what is left over." At this Koshari immediately began to eat.

(Thus in the ceremonial Koshari always grab the food the katsina bring to the people and then demand some themselves, for example biting a piece out of a melon before giving it over. They make imaginary houses to live, lines of ashes with a space left for the door. They enter formally, slamming the door.)

After they had broken fast, Koshari was sent out with a message that the people were to come in. All of the people entered. Everyone, it will be remembered was sick, and they came to wish the Oak Man luck. Iatiku was going to initiate the Oak Man, also Koshari. They sang a song. Iatiku instructed Oak Man to take the corn during the song and stir it with his bare hands into the hot coals. So Koshari did it too. After the corn was parched, Oak Man was to jump into the hot coals, throwing hot coals over his chest and body. (They still initiate in this way. [87] Before this is done they mix some medicine, a plant ground up fresh, with which they paint their bodies. It is called hakanyi, fire.) After this was done it meant he was a member of the altar--the altar belonged to him. Many other songs followed this first song.

"The next thing you are to do is to make wawa (medicine)." First they go after water, getting yellow water (north), blue water (west), red (south), white (east). (The water is not actually colored; this is in the song. The names of the mountains are called for each direction.) [88] Then the song to get herbs for the medicine is sung. Some of the medicine is taken and there is a song-prayer for the power to come to the medicine from the north, east, south, and west. After they finish the water song, they pour the water, a shell full at a time as each direction is named. At one time during the medicine making they have to smoke. Iatiku told Oak Man to roll a cigarette and put honey on the end that goes into the mouth, because this renders the tobacco more powerful, gives it more power to reach out and to be appreciated. Thus, when the medicine man smokes this sacred tobacco mixed with honey representing all food, the smoke goes into the air and is carried by the air to all the people, entering them and healing and nourishing them. Before this for a long time they had known tobacco but they had not known about adding honey to it.

After the medicine is mixed, another song is sung to give medicine to the altar. Eagle feathers are dipped in the medicine and it is sprinkled over the altar. After Oak Man did this he sprinkled medicine in the same way over the audience. Then Koshari brought some ashes and placed them in front of the altar and did the same with the ashes, dipping the tips of the feathers under them and sprinkling them over the people. This lasted all night.

Iatiku then instructed Oak Man to put on the bear paw like a glove and to take the arrowhead and the honani. He did this, holding the honani in his right hand and the arrowhead with the bear paw in his left. All the people moved up to the front, sitting on the ground. He went to each one in turn touching them first on the head, then on the shoulders, the knees, and the feet while the song and prayer went on. Each time a person was touched he would inhale deeply and the Medicine man would blow the spirit of Iatiku toward him. After this he went among the people and sucked the sickness from each in turn, from the chest (over the heart), with his lips. [89] Before he started to do this, Iatiku told him to take some of the medicine and put it over his eyes. This opened his eyes so he could see into them [90] [i. e., the people]. They were all naked. He would then spit up this sickness from his mouth, catch it in the palm of his hand, and cast it off. [91] When he had finished sucking [92] he gave every one a drink from a shell containing medicine, just a mouthful: Koshari did this [93] [i. e., administered the medicine]. It is still done so. [94]

This was not finished till daybreak (4 a. m.). Then the people were told that they might go. A dismissal song is sung for them to go out. Before they were dismissed, Oak Man got up and spoke, saying that Iatiku had said that the altar was to represent her. "We will call it nitranaish [95] shuksts (it will be our mother [Iatiku]). Thus she gives it to us forever, and the chaianyi will have for their purpose the healing of sickness." So the people were told to go and rest.

Iatiku. was still there, so she said to Oak Man, "You know everything now, but I have seen that you need helpers, so you are going, to make other groups (mi'ik) of medicine men." She told him they were to be named: Flint (histian) Chaianyi; Spider (kǎpi'nǎ), [96] Chaianyi; Giant (shkui) Chaianyi. These four, Fire, Flint, Spider, and Giant are the only ones in the tradition. Fire Chaianyi, the Oak Man, was instructed to make altars for them similar to his.

Iatiku told Oak Man the way to select these three men. "If any should be sick and wish for long life and come to you and say they wish to become chaianyi, the first man or woman to say it you are to initiate and give the first altar; the second, the second altar; and the third, the third altar."

Iatiku went on, "There is one other way to take people into your order. During the 4 days of fasting, if anyone enters [your place] you are to take him as your child and initiate him. There is still another way to initiate people into your order. It is through tobacco. If anyone should roll a cigarette in the corner and give it to you without lighting it, you are to take this person and initiate him." [97]

The people learned all about this and they found that this ceremony had cured them. Iatiku told Oak Man to take down all of the altar and to be very careful with it and to pack it away. "You are to leave all this in a room other than the kaach. The honani you are to take to your home where you may watch it and love it and never forget to feed it before you eat a meal."

Then Iatiku said, "Now you will rest, but any time Country Chief wants you to cure his people he will tell you and you must obey him. And if anyone comes to you wanting to be a member of your order, you will tell Country Chief and he will help you arrange it."

Iatiku turned to Koshari and said, "You have done your work faithfully but you are not acting normally enough to be here with the people." He was different from the other people because he knew something about himself, so Iatiku told him to go and live at hakuai'ch [98] (the house of the Sun). "You are to be a help to the Sun. You will be called at times to help here. You are not going to be afraid of anything or to regard anything as sacred. You are to be allowed everywhere." So Iatiku painted him white with black stripes around his body [99] and said, "This is your costume" (pl. 5, fig. 3). She took some of the things from the altar and gave them to Koshari saying, "You will use these." He thanked her but said, "I can make more to it and get what I want." So he went and lives today with the Sun, whom he helps.

WANDERINGS, PART IV

IT happened that a man came and wanted to be a chaianyi. So Oak Man told (him) he would be Kapina chaianyi. Oak Man asked Iatiku what this Kapina was going to represent. Iatiku said he would represent Tiamuni (her husband). Iatiku left it to Tiamuni to say how the altar would be made. So Tiamuni instructed Oak Man to make a tsamai'ya. [100] Tiamuni told Oak Man to gather two ears of corn, one to represent the male (long), the other the female (small). The male was to be named tsamaiya; the female, umahia. [101] The materials needed were the same as for making honani, except that more feathers were necessary. He was to get feathers from as many birds of prey as possible. After this was done Tiamuni came and instructed Oak Man how to make it up and he blew his breath into the corn ear and closed it with cotton. It was made up like the honani except that the "seat" was abalone shell wrapped in cotton. It was then wrapped halfway up from the bottom with buckskin (pl. 13, fig. 2).

When Tiamuni blew in his breath he put in flesh from bashya, "kangaroo mouse." This was the first flesh animal given Nautsiti and Iatiku to eat. It was, therefore, to represent all animal food. This would insure the people of always having meat. If a man wishes to go on a hunt, he should go to his altar as it represents all food animals. Tiamuni, being a male, the breath he blew in represented bravery, initiative, strength, and long life.

Then Tiamuni instructed him how to make the sand painting (ha'atse tsitiă chăn, "earth drawing") for this altar. The drawing was to be made the same as for the honani altar excepting that tracks

of the different game animals are put on the center of the figure of the earth, which is to be gray, and the direction colors for north, south, east, and west are added.

The female umahia represents the "mother" of the people.

So Tiamuni taught him songs different from the ones sung before the altar of Iatiku. This altar was not to cure the sick like that of Iatiku, but was to give strength to the people.

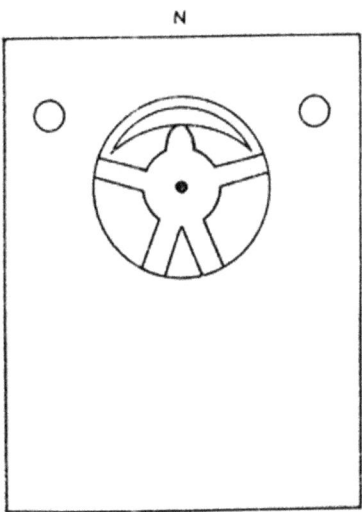

FIGURE 3.--Kapina society altar.

The foundation of this altar is of hoak'a yaoni (sky stone) to represent the sky. The altars in the kiva are always set on the north side in the direction of Shipapu. As one stands facing south, on the right side of the altar is the tsamaiya (male) and on the left is the female (umahia) (fig. 3). The female is like a mother "guardian angel" who represents the female instincts of maternity toward the people and holds them in her affection and heart; the male represents power and virility.

Both were alike, only one was large and one, small. They were more than a foot through and as high as a man or woman. There is nothing back of the altar like that of Iatiku--just the two fetishes and the drawing with the bowl in the middle.

Tiamuni told them to fast for 4 days as Iatiku had done. Everything was done in order as Iatiku had done; Tiamuni was present to give it life. Tiamuni told this medicine man to gather plants for medicine; they must be hardy plants. He was to get oak balls and leaves from dyapi (ironwood?) (rabbit sticks are made from it), leaves from witsthuich (arrows made from it), wishuits (bows and arrows made from it). (Weapons are made from these four trees.) These leaves and oak balls were to be dried and ground to make medicine. Tiamuni told him also to have yucca blades there in a basket. A woman had also [?] stopped to be a chaianyi and she was to help him. Tiamuni told the medicine man that this altar was for work during daylight. He was to fast 4 days, as in Iatiku's instructions, and especially not to eat flesh.

When all was ready, Country Chief went to get Tiamuni. The one to be initiated as chaianyi of this Kapina altar took Tiamuni by the hand and seated him behind the altar. They started singing the first song of the ceremony, this song was to give life to the medicine bowl. There was another song about the trees of the different color-directions. Then the chaianyi got up and with his feathers sprinkled the two fetishes as they came to life. Then the chaianyi brought out the man and the woman who were to be initiated. The chaianyi took some medicine in a shell and gave some to each. Then they passed the yucca blades to Tiamuni (the large variety, hatuni, that gives fruit of seedy brown). "Here is my life," said Tiamuni, "with this (the yucca blades) you will clothe yourself with manliness and with athleticism." So he gave it (the yucca) to the man to be initiated. Tiamuni said, "Here is my mother. You will keep our life stored here and we will be forever dependent on you and nourishment will be from you." So Tiamuni handed the basket to the woman who was to be Kapina chaianyi.

After they had finished with the altar it was time to bring food for the fetishes. So Country Chief told the people and they brought food to the door and offered it to the spirits in the different directions. After they had gone, the ones who were to become chaianyi then ate. The Country Chief notified the people that it was time for them to come in. When it came time to initiate, Tiamuni came in front of the altar, dipped the yucca blades in the medicine which had been mixed and the two to be initiated were brought out to the tsiwaimitiima, the hollow place with altar in kiva. Then came the song to which they were to dance on it. At a part of the song called "héăsh" [fog], Tiamuni struck the man candidate four times on the back with the yucca (during this the woman and man candidates were holding the basket between them). This was done because the basket represented the female fetish. After the man was struck four times, it was the woman's turn. The man held the basket and the woman was struck four times when the "heash" part of the song came. During all this Oak Man was back of the altar singing. This completed the initiation.

So the people were told it was their turn, the ones who had brought feathers as offerings to the two fetishes. All came to the front with their feathers and started to pray. The Kapina chaianyi received the feathers from the people and started to put them in the fetishes, the man chaianyi putting them in the male fetish and the woman, in the female.

When all was finished another song was begun and all who had brought feathers lined up and Tiamuni gave the yucca blades to the Kapina chaianyi, telling him he now knew how to impart the power of the yucca blades. Country Chief came past followed by his two helpers, each in turn holding the basket together with the woman chaianyi, while the male Kapina chaianyi struck each in turn four times on the back. (Nowadays people line up to be in front of the line as the yucca does not hurt so much at first.) That finished the ceremony and the people were allowed to go home with instructions from Tiamuni that the altar was to be cared for, and telling them they now knew the work it had to do. (This altar has nothing to do with curing sickness.)

WANDERINGS, PART V

FOR a long time after this all was well, these two groups of chaianyi did well by the people, but there came another sickness on the people which the chaianyi failed to cure. (Iatiku was still with the people.) So Oak Man thought of making another order of medicine men to be called Flint Chaianyi to help him. It was left to Oak Man from now on to initiate the other orders of medicine men but Iatiku, instructed him to come to her for their names.

Flint Chaianyi was to heal any sickness brought by clouds and lightning. [102] It was to be called Flint but was to combine the power as well of clouds and lightning,--flint is the tangible projectile of the lightning which comes from the clouds.

Three men came to be made chaianyi by Oak Man. So these were to be initiated and given the Flint altar, one exactly like the Fire medicine altar. But the name would be Flint and the songs would be different. But the initiation was not to be different. Everything was followed like getting sticks, etc., from where lightning had struck, 4-day fast, and the meeting was begun in the same way. Each initiate was given honani with the same rites as in the Fire society. These honani were all alike. The fetishes were given life by songs as before. There was initiation with hot coals, as in the Fire society. (Nowadays this is done outdoors.)

The sickness had been caused by a big flood which had made the people ill. The medicine at this altar is mixed in the same way as the other in the ceremony, but is made out of the "heart" of clay concretions that are formed by the wind rolling clay in the arroyos. The centers are removed and ground up with the roots of pŭtru 'ĭst [lightning] (a root which is braided as it grows, representing the lightning). They were also instructed how to paint clouds on the kiva walls (pl. 10, fig. 1). [103] (Acoma is the only pueblo that has these wall paintings.) [104] Then they were instructed how to get power from these paintings. [105] They were to rub their backs against these paintings--against the north wall first. (Nowadays a chaianyi does this before sucking a sick person. Also they sometimes go into the fire to get more power; they dance on the coals.)

Added to the altar was a putruist [lightning stick] representing the lightning. In initiation, Oak Man took this and struck the initiates first on the heart and then on the back giving them the power of lightning. This is added to the hot-coal ceremony. The putruist is made from lightning-blasted pine or spruce.

Flint Chaianyi has a longer bear paw on the left hand than Fire Chaianyi. It reaches to the elbow. One of the three men was made the head chaianyi of the altar and each was to care for his own fetish. Everything was done as before; the people brought food to break the 4-day fast of the chaianyi and the people were cured of their sickness. The Flint society, it must be remembered, is just a help to the Fire society to carry its power further through the power of the clouds and lightning.

When Fire Altar Man was getting his first instructions from Iatiku he was told that he would have the power to take a new-born child and present it to the Sun and give it a name 4 days after birth. This power was given to each successive medicine man. On the fourth day after birth, the father of the child would go to any medicine man, bringing him corn meal with a prayer asking him to present the child to the Sun. On the fourth day, at about 3 a. m., the medicine man comes to the house of the baby. He brings his honani and makes a sand painting [106] on the north side of the room, a painting like the one on his altar. The honani is placed on the "heart" of the altar. He sings prayers as he sets this up and mixes medicine for the child and the family. When the sun is about to come up, he takes the child outdoors, holding it where the sun will shine on it, as it comes up. As the sun rises he prays, gives the baby its name and its clan name. He asks in prayer that the baby may have a long healthy life. He then motions four times from the sun toward the child, bringing the strength of the sun into the child, saying, "Now you have become a member of such and such clan." Then the chaianyi turns to the left (as in kiva leaving) and brings the child back to its home. (It is now a rule that when a man is in a mask dance or in ceremony he always turns to the left.)

When the medicine man gets back to the baby's house, he calls out, "Here comes (whatever name has been given)." The parents reply, "Oh, yes, let him come in." Chaianyi says, "He is coming in, he is bringing food, beads, game, and a long life into his house." As soon as he steps in, the mother takes the child and with four gestures waves inside the food, pots, beads, game, etc., that the child is bringing figuratively to the house. The parents always have food prepared to offer to the altar and to feed the chaianyi. The chaianyi and all of the family come in and eat. Following this the chaianyi makes a departing speech and prayer. He is given some food as a present to take home.

The Giant society was the next to be formed. [107] Thus there were the following medicine societies and in the following order: Fire, Kapina, Flint, Giant. At Acoma there were also Ant society and Eagle society, but these two are not covered by the tradition.

Iatiku was much pleased with her people and the way the various officers and medicine men were functioning. A long time passed and the people were behaving in such a secret way and it was all so solemn, Iatiku thought they should have something public that everyone could enjoy without fasting. So she thought of the clothes that had been presented to the people by the katsina. She called Country Chief to council and told him her plans. She said to him, "Why not call the people to a dance of thanksgiving for the crops and game they have had?" This idea pleased Country Chief much (especially as it came within his province), so he told the people to meet in the kiva. They all met and he instructed them how this affair was to be carried out. (Each person had a katsina costume that had been presented to him.) This dance was to be called paashko. [108] The idea was to get the people away from the continuous solemnity of the secret ceremonies.

Country Chief told the people to make their own songs, that this dance was to be danced by everyone who wanted to dance--boys, girls, men, and women. Katsina dance with just one foot so when the people suggested that they dance like katsina--which was the only dancing they had ever seen--Country Chief said, "No! this is your dance and you must do it a different way." [109] But he knew no way to do it. (This dance is in no sense sacred.) [110] They decided to spend 4 days preparing for the dance, making up the songs and rehearsing. Everyone was happy, full of anticipation; the whole pueblo was stirred up.

So the War captain [Country Chief] kept suggesting that they call Koshari, that he was going to call him. This was because he knew of no new way to dance and he wanted to leave it to Koshari to arrange the dance and instruct the people in it. Koshari had power to do this. Country Chief said to his two helpers, "I'll try out Koshari and see if he will come. He talks a lot and seems to know everything." So he made a prayer stick and prayed and made a cigarette for him. This prayer stick reached Koshari at hakuaich. On the morning of the fourth day Koshari arrived, still painted in stripes, with his hair tied up on top of his head. He asked for Country Chief, "Am I needed here? I have been called to this place." He was brought to the kiva where Country Chief was. Country Chief said, "Yes, I want you here. I believe now that you are real and have power. My people are going to have a dance and I am leaving it all to you to arrange as you may wish." He explained to Koshari the purpose of the dance. Before he had stopped telling him about it, Koshari knew all about it and said, "Yes, I will arrange it for you." So Country Chief told the people that they were to obey Koshari. [111]

Koshari went out, going from house to house telling the people to hurry up and come out. They were much interested in him and obeyed him. He said, "All who want to dance come on to the kiva." He was the one to show them how to paint themselves and put on their costumes. While going from house to house, Koshari spied the drum belonging to the chaianyi. (The drum, of course, was only for a very sacred purpose, [112] but without asking permission Koshari took it.)

He also took the chaianyi's rattle, saying, "This is needed." He was going to have a rehearsal inside the kiva, so he chose two dance leaders, giving to one the rattle, and to the other, who was to sing, he gave the drum.

All the men were lined up. Behind each man he placed a woman and behind each boy, a girl. Then he showed them how to dance, standing in front, lifting both feet, saying, "This is how you will dance (to the men)." He showed the women how to wave their arms in time with the drum, saying, "You will dance thus."

The people who were to be spectators were anxiously waiting outside. Koshari told the drummer to go out first and beat the drum. This he did, all the spectators watching. The singers were sent out next; then the dancers. After they were all up [i. e., out of the kiva] Koshari lined them up in the order they were to proceed to the plaza. Everyone was happy because Koshari made a lot of fun while lining them up, talking backward-- everything he said meant the opposite. (When you talk to a Koshari today this is true: tell him to bring something back and he won't.)

The dance went on all day, though Koshari dismissed them at noon to go home and eat, telling them to come back after eating, which they were only too glad to do, as they were enjoying it very much.

The dance went on all day. When the sun was going down they came out for the last time. For this dance Koshari showed them a new way to dance. This consisted of an arm motion as if pushing aside; this is called kawispăts. "You must always use this when you finish your dances," Koshari told them.

Iatiku was there at the dance. She was much pleased and thought that this public dance was a fine thing. When it was over, Country Chief made a talk. "Koshari has made this dance for us," he said, "This is the way we are to enjoy ourselves and have pleasure." So he thanked Koshari and told him to go home, that he had done well. Koshari said, "Yes, any time you call me I will come. But next time make a much bigger drum and have a lot of rattles." So Country Chief told the people to make bigger drums and more rattles. Koshari called the ones who were going to sing mătaiik, "grapes"; he had pushed them together in a bunch to sing with no order. [113]

Iatiku was pleased that her people were happy. But she wanted to give them still more to enjoy. She knew Flint Chaianyi had a prayer stick dawak [kick stick], which represented the power that makes the Clouds move. She decided to borrow this prayer stick and have the men dance with it. So Iatiku told Flint Man to make this prayer stick and to pray to the Shiwana, "the Clouds," to invite the katsina for their pleasure. (She was thinking the katsina too needed some pleasure.) So Flint Man made a prayer stick and gave it to Iatiku, who gave it to Country Chief, who selected some men to run a race. Iatiku showed them how they were to race with it. They were to kick it along and never to touch it with their hands. [114] First they were to go to the north, then turn to the left to the west, then to the south, then to the east to where they had started in the plaza. The Clouds came up (with the katsina in them) to watch the race. Afterward it rained. The Clouds travel with two of these kick sticks; one with black stripe in middle called tsoyu (belted), the other called k'ashi (white) [115] (pl. 14, fig. 2, a). Flint Chaianyi and Country Chief waited at the goal. The first to enter the plaza would be the winner. So Country Chief took one of these oak prayer sticks and the chaianyi the other. They took them out to the arroyos and prayed. They found this was a very good game and that it brought rain as they expected. (Rain clouds usually come from the west at Acoma.)

Nowadays, at Acoma, the race is run by two teams, chosen from any two kivas.[116]

The medicine man found out the katsina were glad that it had rained and had enjoyed the game. So the men began practicing running. Flint Chaianyi told the runners how to prepare themselves and train. He told them in April to take the leaves from any hard wood and to make a tea to drink, then to take eagle down and tickle their palate so as to vomit the tea, and the medicine would stay inside and make them strong [117] and hardy like the tree. (Nowadays the racers sweat themselves. Water mixed with medicine as above is poured on hot rocks. The medicine man is present and he sprinkles the water while they sing with blanket over door.) All their things were bet on the race: blue, white, and black blankets, etc. They would race every afternoon over a 15-mile course.

Then Iatiku thought of making another game for them called tokiamoti (pl. 14, fig. 2, b). She thought of making this game because she wanted to use the wooden balls. These balls were used by the katsina for making thunder and lightning by striking them together. When they hit, lightning shoots; the rolling is thunder. The game was to be held in the pueblo in the kakati (middle). So Iatiku told Country Chief to ask the katsina next time they came to bring these balls, which they did and gave them as a present to Country Chief. These were presented by Gomaiowish, who taught Country Chief how to play the game. This game was for gambling.[118] They bet one turquoise bead on a game. They found this game very interesting because it was the first game of chance.[119]

Now the men invented a game for themselves to play in kiva. They duplicated the sticks as used in the kicking race, making four such. The sticks are hollow at the end; a pebble is to be hidden in one of the sticks. Two teams are chosen. The team holding the sticks sings a song. The other team then guesses which stick contains the pebble. A couple of referees hold 100 straws each. Rules:

Pick up one stick, an empty one, before picking up one with pebble	Lose five.
Pick up three empty ones	Lose two.

Pick up stick with pebble first	Lose ten.
Pick up two empty ones, then the one with pebble	Guesser gets the sticks..

The one to get all the straws wins. The game is called aiawakutee.

Some of the old men objected to this game, as they had had no instructions to make it. Iatiku did not like it either. The young men made up their own songs with the game and began making up songs about the women and referring humorously to men's wives. The young men got more interested in playing this game in kiva than in attending the ceremonies. They got worse and worse and finally made songs making fun of Iatiku. So Country Chief advised them to stop this. They pretended to do so when he was there, but resumed playing as soon as he was gone. Some of the boys had said that the game was more sure of gaining something for the player than were the ceremonies of Iatiku. This angered Iatiku and she said, "All right, I'll let you go on your own, and see if it is not due to my instructions that all has been going well." She told them she was going to keep quiet and they would not hear from her any more. On saying this, Iatiku disappeared. She told Country Chief that he was to watch his people, that even if the people had made fun of her way of doing, was still going to be their mother and was going to stay at Shipapu and wait for them to come back to her at the end of their lives. This was the first mention of death.

WANDERINGS, PART VI

BEFORE leaving, Iatiku said to Country Chief, "You have made me cry. I feel hurt that I can no longer be with my people. It has been ordered that these eggs which are still left in the basket should be taken by the people till they reach a place called ha'ako (the real name for Acoma today). This is in a south direction. Wherever the echo returns the clearest, they are to search, calling haako! haako! Where the echo comes best will be the right place. When you find this place you are to break one of the eggs. One of these is parrot, the other is crow." She told them to break the parrot egg at haako and to take the other one farther south to kŭyŭpukauwăk, "southwest end." [120]

Even before this Iatiku had told them to move from Shipapu to the south, saying, "You will increase and scatter out." So the people had moved and settled down at kashkachu. (White House). This was where they began playing the game and where famine was to strike them. After the people increased, they did not know how many there were and they did not know how to count them, so the Country Chief, whose business it was to know, asked Iatiku how he might know their numbers. And Iatiku showed him how to count. She spread out her fingers and started to count, beginning with the little finger of the left hand:

isk [121]	1	shi'ĭs[th]	6
du	2	mai'tian	7
chĕm[i]	3	kokomĭsh	8
diă'nă	4	maioku	9
tămŭ	5	kăts	10

Iatiku and Tiamuni disappeared. The people found out that they had done wrong and the katsina and the rulers of the directions found it out also. So the katsina said, "Well, let it go at that, and see if they can run the world by themselves. We will have our Father (Antelope Man) there. But we will let them alone a while and not visit them." So Spring came and it was dry. No clouds appeared. The harvest was very short. So Country Chief went to pray to Iatiku to come back. He made prayer sticks for the katsina, and Antelope Man did the same. They also prayed to the Kopishtaiya, who bring the seeds of all the plants. The chaianyi worked as hard as they could; they set up altars, made prayer sticks, and prayed. But many seasons passed and they heard nothing from the gods. Everything dried up and famine came upon them. Each year things were more scarce, although Country Chief told the people to gather all they could. When this happened, the boys stopped their jokes and once more took part in the prayers, but nothing seemed to help. The people had no power.

There was living at this time a man by the name of Tsaiaiduit. [122] He was a very good and quiet man, who never mixed much with the people and who was like a hermit, living alone with his mother. He was always very careful and saving with crops; he gathered every grain without wasting any and he picked up any he found on the ground. So Country Chief thought of him. Country Chief had tried every other way to call the katsina. He visited Tsaiaiduit and found out he was the only man who still had some provisions. (All of the game was hidden and the hunters could find none.) Country Chief spoke to him, saying, "I have come, my son, I would like to get your help. I know you do not mix much with the people but I know you believe in Iatiku. You were always first in prayers and have always made your offerings faithfully. I know that you will take care of yourself in these things." He told him, "I came to you for help. I want you to call the clouds. Maybe something will work for you. Maybe someone will listen to you. Maybe your prayers are stronger than ours. You have seen that we have tried and failed." But the man answered, "I have no power and nothing to give. I am just a common human." [123] But his mother said to him, "Why don't you receive his words? It may be that the one that gives us life Iatiku) will listen to you. We will depend on your prayers." So the man said, "I do not know that I have any power. My mother has asked me to do as you ask." So Country Chief brought him sacred corn meal, prayer sticks, pollen, beads, tobacco. He took them. Country Chief prayed first and told him to pray with these and that be was counting on him. The man said he did not know where to pray, or whom to ask to help. So Country Chief said, "It is up to you; I can only name the different kivas and the medicine." So Tsaiaiduit asked them how many days were set aside for him and when he was to work. "Four days to prepare," said Country Chief. "When the sun rises the fourth day you are to try." Then Country Chief left him.

The man felt helpless and sorry for himself but soon light came to his mind. He knew a medicine man of the Flint altar, who was quiet like himself, so he went to him, saying, "I come to you. Power has been given to you, so I ask your help." So he told him that Country Chief had left it to him to bring rain. Flint Chaianyi felt sorry for him, and said, "Even I, who have been given power like the other chaianyi, find I can do nothing. But I am going to got myself together and help you." So the chaianyi asked if he wanted help from all the chaianyi of the altar. He replied, "No, just yourself." The chaianyi said, "All right. I will help you." The medicine man told Tsaiaiduit to go to North Mountain. "You are to cut tru'kana (willow) which is still green. You will also cut spruce branches." He taught him a song he was to sing and told him to sing it when he reached the mountain and while gathering spruce. So the man did as told and brought back all that was asked for.

The medicine man was waiting for Tsaiaiduit at Tsaiaiduit's house. When Tsaiaiduit got back, Flint Chaianyi said to him, "This is where you are going to work." The Flint altar was already in place. So the chaianyi met Tsaiaiduit at the door and took his bundle, making a path for him with his cornmeal. The chaianyi told him, "Tomorrow we will purify ourselves by vomiting with medicine."

They kept away from the people. Country Chief was sent to watch and guard the house. Tsaiaiduit's mother was encouraging him all the while. The next day they made prayer sticks and prayed to the North after first praying to Iatiku. Every time they made prayer sticks they would purify themselves. They offered prayer sticks to the West (Wenimats katsina), then to West Mountain, and to all the other powers in that direction. Thus they worked, one day in each direction, till after 4 days they had prayed to all the powers in till the directions. Every night they sang, and every night Country Chief watched the house until the songs were finished. All the people knew what was going on and all were helping with their prayers.

When the sun came up on the fourth day, Tsaiaiduit dressed up like the katsina Tsaiaiduit but without mask. He made up his own decorations. He had been named after this katsina, hence the costume. So Country Chief and officers brought him out first to the north, then to the west, south, and east. The chaianyi stayed in the house singing the same song as the dancer. Tsaiaiduit danced and sang on each side of the Plaza. His mother encouraged him before he left. He was a very good singer and dancer. Everyone came to see him and the people all encouraged him; many of the women cried in sympathy for him. But he was very brave and did not slacken his singing or dancing till he had finished his four songs. While he was dancing, Country Chief was urging the people to stay with him in the plaza and to continue to encourage him. Tsaiaiduit was escorted back to his house to rehearse four more songs.

When he came, out the second time a very small cloud appeared in the South. Iatiku, also the katsina, felt sorry for Tsaiaiduit. They had seen him working alone, so they decided to answer his prayers. While he was dancing the second time, in the south the small cloud began to grow. When he was dancing on the south side of the plaza, it began to rain very hard, but Country Chief did not let the people go, home. [124] Tsaiaiduit kept on dancing in the rain. After finishing his second dance, he was escorted back home to break his fast. After eating, he came out the third time and it was still raining and the people stayed on. So he returned and came out the fourth time. It continued to rain for 4 days and 4 nights. Country Chief thanked Tsaiaiduit very much and said a prayer for him as he released him from his duties. So the people even today believe that the common people are the last resort and have the most power. If something should happen and the medicine men could not help, the final resort would be a common man. [125]

This rain did not bring a large harvest but gave them a lot of wild food plants which they gathered and saved for the winter. (The rain came too late for the crops.) Game again appeared. This was the reawakening of the katsina and afterward they continued to visit the people when they were asked. When the Kopishtaiya were called, they came also. So they continued having their pleasure dances and the games that were given them and for a long time they quit the gambling game.

WANDERINGS, PART VII

ALL was going well for a long time until again some one who had the game brought it back, and the young people began again to play, although the old folks scolded them. Now one time the katsina came to visit, bringing presents and rain. That night after the katsina left, one of them stayed on in the village, while the boys returned to the kiva to play their game. There were many players in the kiva. So the katsina went in without being noticed, back of the crowd, and watched them play and heard them talk and sing. One of the gamblers got more fresh and started to sing a song which grew more and more disrespectful, and some men started to dance like katsina. They burlesqued the dances and they mocked [126] the peculiarities of some of the katsina (some were bow-legged, some had off-set lips). Finally one said, "Is this the way the clouds look?"

Finally the katsina went out and called to the other katsina. When the people heard it they were startled, saying, "Who was that went out?" But they found it was a real katsina. Some said they thought they had seen the real katsina go out. They were frightened, saying, "A katsina has seen us mock the katsina." This katsina took the story back to Wenimats. There was a man who was not in the kiva at the time they were mocking. He was on his way in when he met the katsina on the roof of the kiva. When he entered he asked, "What was that katsina doing here?" They kept quiet when they found this was a real katsina, and, knowing they had made a mistake, they kept quiet. So they quit playing and went home, feeling heavy-hearted.

When the katsina got back to Wenimats, he yelled and everyone was filled with excitement and rushed out. He told the katsina chief what he had seen and other katsina were listening and even before he finished telling, some of them began to get angry. Katsina Chief tried to calm them, saying, "Wait, don't get excited!" But they were all enraged. Gomaiowish took the lead on the side of the angry ones. He said, "I am going to tell them that we are coming to visit them." Katsina chief told him not to go, but he went anyway. Katsina Chief urged that there be no hasty action and tried to get them to settle the matter by discussion, if possible, without harming anyone.

Just after midnight that night in the pueblo, the people heard Gomaiowish crying out in the plaza, saying, "I have brought you a message. The katsina are going to visit you and they will bring you presents. They will bring you everything you need, hunting sticks, clubs, so wait for them, make prayer sticks and be prepared for them and prepare a feast for them." Everyone got up, not knowing what was happening. They heard Gomaiowish giving a strange yell they had never heard before. However, they understood his instructions. His yell sounded like crying. The people were frightened, wondering why Gomaiowish was so different. Those who had been in the kiva mocking were the only ones who could guess the reason. They got together and decided that their burlesque must have been the cause. No one went to bed, but stayed up, questioning one another. Gomaiowish left but returned just before sun-up.

When be came the second time they saw that he had clubs and hunting sticks in his hands. Antelope Man (head chaianyi [127] and Father of the katsina) painted himself up and put on the full costume in which he had always met the katsina. The Country Chief and his officers did likewise, and went forth to meet Gomaiowish. Antelope Man said to Gomaiowish, "Have you come, my son?" Gomaiowish replied, "Yes, my father, I have come. I have come to tell you that the katsina are anxious to come and visit you. They will be here a little after noon. They are going to bring presents to your people." Antelope Man tried to talk with Gomaiowish as usual; all the other people were looking on, but Gomaiowish would not come near them. So Antelope Man asked why he did not step up and tell him why the katsina were coming. He told Gomaiowish to stop, and offered him a cigarette. 'But Gomaiowish made excuses, saying he did not want to smoke because tobacco made one lazy, made the joints crack, and made the eyes water so one could not see a deer when hunting. They tried other ways to get him to stop and talk and to placate him. But Gomaiowish, being the leader of the angry katsina, would not be placated. So Antelope Man asked Gomaiowish to give him the stick he had brought: "Was he not going to give it away? You are my friend, why don't you present it to me?" Country Chief came near and tried to calm Gomaiowish. He caught, hold of him, but Gomaiowish got very angry and hit him with the club. Other men jumped on Gomaiowish and grabbed him. Antelope Man ordered them to bring him to the kiva, hoping that there they could humor him and quiet him down. But Gomaiowish broke loose. He was faster than any of the men, who pursued him in vain. They had taken away his clubs and hunting sticks.

So Gomaiowish went back to Wenimats and brought added complaint, telling that the people had taken away his clubs and sticks. He exaggerated what they had done. He persuaded the other katsina that the people were very wicked, and added fuel to their anger. The katsina leader Tsitsanits tried again to quiet them but they would not listen. All the katsina left in a large band although Tsitsanits tried to stop them and send them back. The people at White House knew there was something wrong, and they all got busy making prayer sticks and praying to the katsina. But the prayer sticks, even when they reached the katsina, were not received. The katsina ran right over Tsitsanits, who was injured trying to stop them; they were on the war path. Before long the people at White House could hear the katsina coming, yelling in the same way they had heard Gomaiowish yell. Country Chief called all the men together. He told the people not to do anything to the katsina. "If they are going to harm us, let us do as they like. Maybe this is to be our punishment. I know that we have been doing wrong." The two sons of the Sun man [Masewi and Oyoyewi] were present as common men; they did not think anything serious was due to happen.

The katsina brought clubs and they had picked up sticks of hard wood, and broken branches off the trees. They were all very angry. They did not pause as they came to the village but came right in by the back way, all in a bunch, and began striking the people with their clubs and killing many of them. The Sun twins rushed to their house. They saw that things had become very serious. They saw their people were being rapidly killed and they got angry toward the katsina. So they started putting on the costumes their father had given them and painted each other as their father had shown them, and put on their quiver with bow and arrows. They intended to fight back at the katsina. The people had made no attempt to defend themselves. The Twins selected the largest bunch of katsina in the plaza and gave the yell their father had taught them (through which they were to get power from the Sun). They knew they were not to use the hunting stick ordinarily, but they decided this was the necessary occasion. After giving their yell, each one let fly a hunting stick at the katsina in the plaza. The sticks killed all the katsina in the plaza, decapitating them and scattering the others in every direction. The Twins killed all the katsina but Tsitsanits the leader, who was with Country Chief, trying to calm down the katsina. They then captured Gomaiowish, berating him: "It is because of you that our people have been killed. you are looking for trouble, so you will have it." Whereupon they tied him and castrated him. Then Gomaiowish confessed and said, "Oh, it is you! Please forgive me!" He knew who the Twins were from their prayers.

When the katsina leader saw that all the katsina had been killed, all of a sudden he became afraid and said, "I think we have done something wrong, else by whose power has this been done?" By that Tsitsanits meant that both sides had been wrong. This was the first time they had seen death. When Tsitsanits asked by whose power it had been done, the Twins stepped forward, saying, "We are the ones. It had to be done. We stood up for the people. We confess that we understand that the katsina are sacred to us. But it has been held also that the katsina on their part should care for the people." All the rest of the people were terror-stricken, as what had happened was very mysterious. They came out from where they were hiding and gathered where Country Chief was, with the Twins and Tsitsanits and Gomaiowish.

As soon as the elder twin finished telling why they had fought back, Tsitsanits understood and knew that it was their father Masewi. So Tsitsanits stepped up to him and put his arms around him and confessed for the katsina that they had done wrong. So Country Chief stepped up to Masewi and said, "You have performed this miracle. Why should it be so hard and so serious as all this? Forgive us all! Can you bring the katsina back to life for our sake? We all understand that it is also by them that we have lived and been happy." So the elder twin spoke to the katsina leader, asking him if what Country Chief had said was true. If they brought them back alive, there was not to be any more killing and they should not become angry. The katsina leader said that he had confessed for them and Country Chief had said what was true. So the elder Twin said, "I also understand that this should never have happened. We also feel very sorry for the katsina, whom we have depended upon. We are going to try to do what you have asked. If our power works, maybe they will be with us again."

So the Twins went among the scattered katsina and, picking up their heads, placed them back in place. Their father (Sun) had given them "jackrabbit ears" (peschwipen), an herb. They rubbed this medicine on the necks of the katcina to connect their heads again and on their chests they placed their staff with the arrowhead (as they had been instructed to do to bring animals back to life). Some of them came back to life after this and quickly got strong, others recovered slowly, and a few did not come to life at all. The Twins worked over them all day till sundown. Country Chief sent the people away while they were doing this, telling them it was not good for them to see what was happening. The chaianyi helped the Twins, but all they did was to follow the Twins' instructions. So after they had done the best they could and had brought back to life all those they could bring back, Country Chief confessed to the katsina that it was the people's fault that this trouble had happened. Tsitsanits replied that the katsina had also made a mistake, and were equally at fault. So to protect both sides he decided that the katsina should not come any more, as they might get angry again. "You will not see us any more, but we will still help you from Wenimats and we will always be waiting for you there. You have received presents of the costume of the katsina. From now on you are going to imitate us. In that way we will help you from Wenimats. You have seen how we, are painted up, you have seen how we are dressed (pl. 12, fig. 2). You know how to make our prayer sticks. Go through the ceremony like this and we will help you spiritually. When you have picked out the costume of the katsina you are to represent, his power will come to you and attach itself while you represent him."

So Country Chief replied, saying, "How can this be made real? We are not appointed to do this." Tsitsanits replied, "Well, I guess you will have to be initiated. In this way you will really represent the katsina." So Tsitsanits laid down the word that he was to be called to teach them how to carry this out and to initiate the people so they could learn to be katsina. Then Masewi asked if this was all. The kachina leader said, "Yes." Masewi said, "This is not all for you yet. You will receive punishment and you will have to fast for three 10's of the times the sun comes up. At the end you will all become really reborn. After this is done we will regard you as we have done before." The elder Twin said that at the end of this time he would come with his brother to Wenimats. Everyone felt sorry for each other and felt very bad. So they gathered and the people brought prayer sticks to the katsina and both sides confessed their wrongdoing and said prayers for each other. Then the katsina left. When they got back to Wenimats, they all died again. For these 30 days they were just alive enough to be able to realize their punishment. [128] Tsitsanits took care of them during this time.

Country Chief asked Masewi and Oyoyewi if they could bring the people alive, and they said, "Yes, we can." So all the bodies were brought into the plaza. They did with them as they had done with the katsina, but none of them came to life. The Twins had also made a mistake. Their father had seen what they had done and had taken away all the power of their medicine staff and arrowhead after they had finished with the katsina. And the hunting sticks had no more power. This is why they could not bring any of the people back to life. So Masewi and Oyoyewi said, "Well, we have failed. What is to be done now?" Country Chief and the chaianyi said that it had been laid down that, if anything like this happened, certain rules were to be followed. "Iatiku said that at some time we would come to the end of life. Maybe this is what has happened." So the medicine men said that they would take care of that. So they painted (pl. 15, fig. 2, a) the faces of the men and the women [129] [i. e., the medicine men [130] prepared the dead for burial which was to take place the day after death, thus inaugurating the funeral ritual, [131] part of which is described at this point in the narrative, as follows.] Before the chaianyi leaves, as many different kinds of food as possible are procured and offered. A fire stick (poker) and an arrow point are placed on the floor and for 4 days after death the soul of the dead person is fed a little after each meal. After 4 days a medicine man is called in to put the family through the forgetting [132] ceremony (pl. 15, fig. 2, b). [133] He is given prayer sticks by the family. He sweeps up the sand painting, and takes out the fire stick and the arrow point and buries them, [134] so the breath [135] of the dead person is removed from the house.

The medicine men remembered how Iatiku had showed them the sand painting of the figure of the earth, with the head to the east, so they thought that probably meant the body should be returned to the earth with the head in that direction, and the feet in the direction the sun goes down. So this is the way the medicine men planted the bodies of their people, so that they would be reborn. The word "plant" is used in this sense in burials.

WANDERINGS, PART VIII

AFTER this the people began to quarrel. They found many new bad words[136] to use against each other. Fights and feuds arose. They did not like each other much any more. They had heard what had been said between Country Chief and Tsitsanits, and that the katsina leader was coming back to teach the people how to act in the supernatural manner of the katsina. But some people wore afraid. They were afraid that if they made a mistake and did not fast just right they would have to pay with their life. [137] But others said everything would be all right. "Let us do as we are asked, and learn to carry on as they want us to," they said. So the people, that, did not wish to see that day come, packed up and left in small bands, or perhaps just man and wife would go away. It is not known where they went and they were never heard of any more. (This may account for the other tribes of Indians; but this is not in the tradition.) Those willing to take instructions from the katsina leader stayed.

So they waited for the day when the katsina were to be reborn, making a tally mark each day till they got three 10's. When the 30th day was approaching, Antelope man called all of his people together and told them what he and Tsitsanits had talked about--the katsina being reborn and that the people were to help in their rebirth and still believe in them. So the people made prayer sticks and brought them to the altar of Antelope man, who took them and prayed to the katsina, asking them to come and visit his people. When the 30 days were up, Masewi and Oyoyewi went to Wenimats and with their prayers gave new life to the katsina. When they got to the top above Wenimats they cried out, saying, "All clouds in the north, all clouds in the west, all clouds in the south, all clouds in the east that have been asleep all this time, come awake!" And the katsina awoke. Also those who had been asleep in Wenimats came awake. The clouds rested because they had no one to pray to them while the katsina slept. Thus all the katsina awoke in good health. (The Kopishtaiya and Koshari and all the rulers were affected when the katsina were killed. They are all partners.)

Antelope Man's prayer sticks were already there and were received by the katsina leader. The katsina took them and prayed to the people and smoked the cigarettes to reestablish contact. Tsitsanits told the katsina they were not to go to the village any more. He sent Gomaiowish to tell the people that he (Tsitsanits) was coming alone on the fourth day to initiate them (tsi'mǎ'ǎwǎ, "to imitate," to give them the strength and right to act the katsina way.) Gomaiowish took the message to the people. He was in a very good humor and told them that the katsina leader was to come alone in 4 days, and for them to wait and purify themselves and prepare a feast for his coming. They understood that they were all going to be initiated.

On the fourth day Tsitsanits came. Antelope Man's altar was all set and everything was ready for him. Gomaiowish came along with Tsitsanits and brought a lot of feather down. All the people went into the kiva and Tsitsanits came with Gomaiowish. The song began. The people were brought up one at a time and Tsitsanits struck them four times with the yucca. [138] The Gomaiowish, who held them while they were being struck, tied feather down on their heads. They were then given advice by Tsitsanits as to how to make masks. They were to duplicate the ones they had seen the katsina wearing. "You have seen the feathers, you have seen how they are painted, and how they wear their costumes. You will do the same way and this you are to carry on into the future as long as there is life." He instructed them to fast 4 days, 8 days, or 12 days, according to what they were doing. During these fast days they were not to touch any woman, and were to purify themselves every day by vomiting. Four days they were to fast and purify their systems by vomiting, on the fourth day to pray to Wenimats, on the fifth day still fasting to bring the masks to the kiva. Now they are ready making new dance songs and fixing masks, painting them, etc., making new equipment. On the eighth day the representatives (katsina chaianyi) [i. e., the persons impersonating the katsina] come. They dance a day and a half and the next day they are sent back to Wenimats. From then on, 8 days more of fasting. No mixing With people, no women. They start eating, though, the day they come out On the fourth day. All this was laid down as rules and all of the people understood them. Some of the people were not satisfied go because they had no power, having been afraid to participate; others were quite satisfied.

After all this was done, Antelope Man thought of trying it out to see how it would work. So the men who were willing to take part met in the kiva. Country Chief instructed the men to make masks, saying that they had to be brought to life before they could be used. "The mask you will make will belong to yourself. Name it for whatever katsina you want to represent." They tried many different skins but they made the best ones of buffalo skin (they were tough and heavy). Those made of buckskin did not look well and had to be made over, It took a long time to make this first set of masks. Some of the men laughed at those who could not make them and many got discouraged and left. Some made very funny masks but they persisted. They sewed the buffalo skin in the shape of a mask. They found it was best to fill them with dry earth and tamp it down, giving them a smooth shape. It took a long time to dry them. The next work was to paint them, but they did not know just where to get the paint. They had to do a lot of experimenting before they were finished. But they could do anything with them because they were not yet sacred. However, they fixed them as nearly as they could to represent the katsina they wanted. They helped one another and in this way they got some finished. "It will be up to our fathers, the chaianyi," they said, "They are the ones who know better than we what to do."

So the men who were to take part made prayer sticks which they gave to Country Chief to present to the chaianyi, asking their aid. Country Chief went to Flint Chaianyi and Fire Chaianyi. That night the chaianyi took the prayer sticks and said they would help. They set the time for the fourth night; then they would help to bring the masks alive so as really to represent the katsina. All waited the coming of the fourth day. The chaianyi were preparing their altars during these 4 days. When all was ready, their songs were finished. The men who had made masks to be brought alive were waiting in the kiva. Word was sent them to bring them to the various chaianyi altars.

The chaianyi went through their ceremonies and gave life to the masks, just as they had done to the fetishes on their altars. They named the masks for the katsina each represented. No one but the medicine men was present at the altars; the men to whom the masks belonged were waiting in the kiva. When the chaianyi had finished giving life to each mask, they would blow it to the owner and then give it to him, saying, "This is now real and it has the same power as the real katsina. You must take good care of it and not neglect it, and most of all, this is going to be secret from this day on. This means that the children and the ones who are not initiated must not know about this and the dancers are not real katsina. This must be hidden from them. Only the women who have become grandmothers (old) shall know of this. (Now all the boys of 12 or 15 know about it, and even the little girls, just as they know about Santa Claus.)

When all this had been done, Antelope Man said, "Let us try it out now. Let us start to work and prepare." He instructed the men to follow the rules that Tsitsanits had given them,--4 days' fasting and so on. They did this and on the fourth day went into the kiva for the first time. While in the kiva they made prayer sticks with which to call the power of the real katsina whom they were to represent. (It had taken a long time to make all these preparations and the earth had become dry, since the katsina naturally had not appeared.)

For 4 days and nights they made songs similar to those that had been sung by the katsina. They were to imitate the katsina in every way they could. They practiced singing and dancing the way the katsina did but as yet without mask and without painting up. Came the fourth day and all had gone well. In the morning they sent out the man who was to represent Gomaiowish. He took his mask, concealed in his blanket, into the country where he was out of sight. He had paint with him to paint himself. He was accompanied by one of the officers of Country Chief, who was to guard him, He painted and dressed himself up in the costume of Gomaiowish. He had with him the prayer sticks he had made, and, placing the mask in front of him facing west (toward Wenimats), he started to pray: "I am praying to the real Gomaiowish. I have made a mask (shpitso, "likeness") similar to yours. I know you are giving it your power so I ask also that the power of your body and your mind be placed into my body and my mind. Even though I am a common human and you are real, help me represent you as you would like me to do. Help me to represent you really." So he took the mask and slipping it over his head, he said, "You that are real, clothe me!" Then he gave the cry of Gomaiowish, saying, "Now I hope to represent you so that my people may go on believing in the katsina." Then he went toward the village, singing a song. It was just sunrise when he reached the pueblo. The War chief's helper, who had been guarding him, kept out of sight.

Gomaiowish went into the plaza. Country Chief, Antelope Man, and the chaianyi knew, of course, that he was coming. Antelope Man went through the welcome [ritual], just as he had done with the real katsina. All the other officers also welcomed him. Gomaiowish told the officers that the katsina were coming to visit them; he said that it was Gaiya katsina (Mixed katsina, i. e., all the different kinds of katsina). This group still comes. [139]

While Gomaiowish was in the plaza, the other katsina impersonators were out in the country, hidden from the pueblo. They were putting on their masks and costumes, each one praying to the katsina he was representing and talking like that katsina. Then they started toward the pueblo, singing.

Soon the people heard them. The children and uninitiated were much afraid, as they did not know whether or not the katsina were going to kill people again. They were trembling from their recollections. So Country Chief cried out and told the people that the katsina were visiting them, and for them to be polite, to quit playing and pay attention. When the katsina came in sight all the people as usual brought out sacred corn meal and made a path for them into the pueblo. They said prayers that they made up themselves. Antelope Man went forth to meet them and spoke to them in the same words he had used in greeting the real katsina. He welcomed them into the plaza. He led them in a row to the north side of the plaza where they always danced first. The officers had prepared things for them in the kiva where they were to be taken to rest after the dance. So they danced the katsina dance. All was done in direct imitation of the real katsina. They danced four times in the north, west, south and east. After this they were brought into the kiva to rest.

In the west side of the kiva, skins of different animals were laid out to form a bench-skins of lion, buffalo, or bear. The dancers took off their masks and placed them on these skins. Country Chief and his officers had tobacco ready and gave all the dancers a smoke. The dancers prepared the songs they were to sing next. Each time they put on the masks to go out again, they would repeat the words they had said the first time. They went out the second time and danced four times as before in the plaza. It was now about mid-day, so they went in again to rest. [140] Country Chief announced that the people should also go and rest, that they were to stay in their houses and not come out until the katsina came out. The old women who knew about the dancers brought in food for them. [141] When food was brought in,

Antelope Man stood up and offered it first to the real katsina, then to the masks on the bench. After a short while, the dancers were told to break their fast. Since the night before at midnight they had not been allowed to drink any water.

During the time the dancers were in the kiva the old women who knew that the dancers were men] would bring presents to any dancer they selected and tell him to present them to the household they named. The dancer would then have to remember and make these presents. Each time they came out, the dancers would bring out some of these gifts and present them. (After the third dance these gifts are presented.)

When they came out the fourth time, the sun was setting. They presented the people with more things, and the dance was over. Antelope Man told the people to bring prayer sticks and place them in a basket in the plaza. When this was done, Antelope Man gave this basket of prayer sticks to Gomaiowish to take with him. After the last dance was over, the dancers made presents as the real katsina had done, taking off all their costume except the mask, and presenting it to members of their own household or to the women that knew [about the dancers], so they would get it back. Then one by one as they disposed of their clothes, the katsina would run off over the desert shouting. The shouts grew fainter as the katsina strung out over the desert and disappeared in the distance. Gomaiowish took along the basket of prayer sticks.

(When they reach the place where they are to unmask, they lift the masks half off--just over the eyes--then take some prayer sticks from the basket and go off by themselves to pray. Each one says, "Now, I believe that you have finished your work. Go back happily to Wenimats! Take with you all which belongs to you and everything that is sacred to you. Let me not be troubled, by your power returning to haunt me in my dreams." Then he takes off his mask and motions four times [142] to Wenimats, saying, "Let me return to my people like a common human. Do not blame me for what I have been doing. Lot nothing wrong happen because I have imitated you. But lot me have good health, long life, and the gifts you have brought." Then they bury the prayer sticks.--There is a big crevice at Acoma where today prayer sticks are thrown down.--Then they take off the feathers that are on the masks and put the masks in shape to carry home. They wait until dark when they scatter out and return, one at a time, from different directions. Then they go to kiva and turn in the masks.)

Antelope Man thanked the men who had taken part and told them all had gone well, but that they were to be continent for 8 days. These were the instructions to Antelope Man from the real Tsitsanits. If anyone broke these rules, even after going through all this hardship, he would not got any of the blessings for which he had asked; he might even shorten his life and die.

WANDERINGS, PART IX

AFTER this, all went well and it began raining and rained at frequent intervals. Everything went on all right and during that summer and fall the people had plenty of everything. The people were still at White House.

In the winter Antelope Man though of trying out the Kopishtaiya, Country Chief called out that the people should make prayer sticks to call the Kopishtaiya. So, after vomiting for 4 days, the men who were to take part met again in kiva. They made prayer sticks (pl. 14, fig. 1) and prepared the masks. [143] (There are no seeds in the Acoma Kopishtaiya masks as at Laguna.) [144] They worked for 4 days in kiva. They made songs different from the katsina songs. They were not songs for dancing but for manliness (hachtsia).

After 4 days in kiva, the impersonators left at midnight and went out toward the east, taking their masks and costumes with them; they painted up in kiva before leaving. They went out into the country away from the people. (One of the Kopishtaiya is female, [145] although impersonated by a man.) Country Chief told the people that on the fourth day they were to expect the Kopishtaiya to visit them from the east.

The Kopishtaiya impersonators got ready just as the katsina impersonators had done. But their prayer sticks were different, being made of hard wood to represent masculinity. They were painted differently and had different feathers. These men went out in pairs in different places in the east to hide. They dressed and prayed, asking the Kopishtaiya to help them. They adopted the yell and accent of the Kopishtaiya they were to represent. They were instructed to be sure to come near the pueblo in pairs and to meet just before sun-up, so they could enter just before sunrise. It was very cold and as soon as the men were dressed they started running to keep warm. When they got together near the pueblo, they all went in together. Antelope Man acted as before, opening the road with corn meal. (They come in pairs, they run and turn back to keep warm, run and turn back, shouting the while.) [146]

When the Kopishtaiya first came, they brought all kinds of evergreen trees, leaving them in the plaza for the people to make a tea of them and purify themselves. Some of the real Kopishtaiya, when they came, showed manliness by bringing cactus on their backs, others carried big chunks of ice. (Anyone wanting bravery will squeeze up against the Kopishtaiya with the cactus so as to give him manliness.) Kopishtaiya still do this. The real Kopishtaiya got real snow to scatter around. Now they bring cactus fluff to represent snow.

The Kopishtaiya were led into the pueblo just before sun-up. They planted all that they had brought and distributed seeds to the people. The people would come up and break some pieces from the evergreen boughs, bring them home and boil them to purify themselves with the decoction. As soon as the sun appeared, the Kopishtaiya left the pueblo. Their spirits, however, remained in the kiva for 4 days; the people were to care for and feed them these 4 days. (Nowadays the Kopishtaiya go into the kiva. They do not send their masks away and take the power from them, but bring them still vitalized to the kiva for the 4 days. It is not told in tradition that the altar was set up during this time, as is done now. During these 4 days, they take food and feed the masks, and when they smoke they give it first to the masks. They also make prayer sticks. On the fourth day the masks are taken out secretly with the prayer sticks. When they reach the country they place the masks facing east, saying, "It is time for you to return to Hakuoikucha-ha. Take back what belongs to you. Do not haunt me. Do not take from me the seeds you have brought or the blessings of manliness." Then the four motions to the east are made, and they say, "Now go and return." The prayer sticks are planted. Then the feathers are taken from the mask and put in order, and the mask has become devitalized. Then they bring the masks back to kiva. Antelope Man receives them and bids them good will, telling them that all has gone well. Then he says a prayer and allows them to go. (For 12 days they must keep away from women. If the rule is broken, their life will be shortened and prayers will not be answered.)

Everything went well and during the winter there was plenty of snow, which helped them catch game. Weapons were not strong at this time, so the snow was a help.

WANDERINGS, PART X

A long time passed, and there were more and more members in the katsina and Kopishtaiya group. Antelope Man gave all of them authority to bring in others to be initiated. They had this authority for, like the chaianyi, they were agents of supernatural power. So Antelope Man would call in different men at different times and tell them secretly what to do. He revealed to them how things were done and asked if they would become members. He would relate everything that had happened, [147] how the people had done wrong, and how they are now imitating the real katsina, who can no longer come in person. Antelope Man would advise the initiate not to take this lightly, not to mock, but to believe. He told them the men who represented the katsina had power and had the right to kill any person who joked about them or mocked them. He told them they should not tell anyone not initiated that so-and-so is a katsina. Thus many men came and wished to become members of the katsina group.

A long time passed and many children grew up. Men who wished to become katsina were brought into kiva to learn from those who were already members. They were instructed in making masks, prayer sticks, songs, and prayers. The men who came in would select someone to teach them. Usually relatives would instruct relatives. Country Chief would take sacred corn meal and go to a member of the society, [148] bringing one or two boys whom he wished to initiate, saying to the member he selected to reach them, "I have brought you a son (or sons) (giving name and clan). You are to be their father. You are to teach them the secrets of your society and you are to help them make their masks and see that they make no serious mistakes." Country Chief again asked the chaianyi to give life to the new masks that were made, which was done as before. Everything followed the same course except that new members were initiated out in the country where they put on their masks, by the member chosen to do the initiating. (The initiator hits the initiate hard four times on the back. After the new member is struck he is supposed to yell like a katsina. In this way a man is initiated into the society for life. New members are given the same privileges as old members.)

Country Chief saw there was too much work in distributing the gifts so he thought of calling on the Koshari. He asked two chaianyi to represent Koshari. He gave them tobacco and corn meal, asking them to represent Koshari, telling them, "You are to give cigarettes to whomever you wish to select to be Koshari." So the chaianyi took the cigarettes that were given them by Country Chief to trap some men. They went from man to man, saying, "Maybe you would like a smoke?" Instead of giving a smoke to the man who accepted, the chaianyi trapped him. They caught two men in this way and notified Country Chief that these two men were to be initiated.

When Country Chief was ready for these two men, he told the chaianyi to bring them. Country Chief and the chaianyi told them what to do to represent Koshari. The men did not like it and tried to back out. But they were told, "You have been caught by the sacred tobacco and unless you go on with this, you will be haunted by the Koshari whose spirit was in the smoke." So the men thought it best to go on with it. The katsina were to come the next day, so the two young men were brought before Country Chief, who had told the chaianyi to tell the young men to come down into the kiva head first. (That is why they talk backward.) The men did this as best they could. Country Chief had previously prepared medicine which he set before them. He had already worked with the songs and prayers. The chaianyi sang the songs which they had prepared. Each time when a certain part in the song was reached, some of the medicine was sprinkled over the two initiates. After the songs, the chaianyi took the two men and (before they started singing they had taken off all their clothes) painted their faces with white clay and with black circles around their eyes and mouths and then their bodies with black horizontal stripes. Their hair was tied standing up in two bunches, just like the real Koshari. These bunches of hair represented the clouds. The chaianyi had skinned two small birds called shuti [Canyon wren] and had left the hearts in. These had been dried and were fetishes. They also prepared two other birds called shpati (mocking birds), which were hung about their neck as a necklace. This fetish was to give them power to talk fast and chatter and mimic like the mocking bird. In this way the two men were initiated.

They were to be heads of the Koshari. They were to initiate each his eldest son and anyone who wished to become a member. The chaianyi told them they were to represent the real Koshari, who had the habit of going wherever they pleased, and they would be allowed to go even in the most sacred places. "You will also have the power of a chaianyi. Even if the chaianyi has made medicine, you can go in and take it without permission and go out and cure anyone you wish with it." (Nowadays the Koshari will sometimes go to the medicine bowl, suck up some of the medicine, and administer it to the patient through his mouth.) The chaianyi told the men they were to know no sadness and were to know no pain even if hurt. They were to know no sickness. (If someone in a household is unhappy or sick frequently they prefer to call on a Koshari rather than on a medicine man.)

The chaianyi also made one honani for the two of them; all others later could use it. It was passed to the one first initiated as he was to be head of the Koshari. This ceremony took all night. By this time Gomaiowish had come bringing the message that the Koshari were Coming. When they heard him in the plaza, the Koshari rushed out and climbed up on the housetop yelling. When they saw Gomaiowish, they jumped down and were the first to meet him. They asked him, "Maybe you want something here?" Gomaiowish said, "I want Antelope Man and Country Chief." "Well, we will get them." The Koshari found Antelope Man and Country Chief, and told them that someone wanted to see them and to wait in the plaza. Country Chief and Antelope Man now met Gomaiowish and went on with their ritual, while the Koshari stood around making jokes. As was the custom, County Chief told the message Gomaiowish had brought, by crying it up the street. The Koshari came behind mocking him, twisting his statements, and reversing the meaning.

Then the katsina came and the Koshari rushed out ahead of everyone to meet them. On meeting them they asked if they were the katsina. They said yes, so the Koshari began sprinkling corn meal and leading them to the pueblo. Everything followed in the usual way, but this time there was a larger group of dancers. The Koshari acted as interpreters for the katsina to the people. The katsina used sign language that the Koshari understood. (Now they are not so secret and speak to them.) The katsina never speak. The Koshari took the presents from the katsina and distributed them to the people, so the people would not see the katsina too closely. They danced all day. Toward the last dance (the day went as before) the katsina were to throw up gifts. The Koshari saw the people were crowding up too near the katsina so they thought of making a boundary line that the people were not to cross and they told the people that was their trap. If any stepped over the line they would take him and make him a Koshari. In this way they kept the people back. This line was made of ashes. They were always very careful to destroy the line after each dance. All went well, the sun was setting and the customary ceremony of praying took place, and the katsina left. The dancers went out to the hiding place and unmasked with the same ceremonies as before and returned the masks to the kiva.

This is the way the katsina are still represented in the pueblo.

WANDERINGS, PART XI

FOR a long time it went on thus and all was well. Sometime afterward, a sickness fell upon the people at White House and for the first time sickness brought death to many people. The population decreased rapidly. The chaianyi called this sickness ushporoni. It was a disease with blisters all over the body (smallpox?). The chaianyi did their best to cure it, but it was too much for them. The people grew very unhappy, as they were dying off fast and they did not go through the proper burial ceremonies. When a person died they just wrapped him up and the family buried him. The Twins, Masewi and Oyoyewi, were the only ones who did not get sick. This was probably because of the power of their father. They tried their power on the sickness, but it did not always work. So they tried harder and harder each time until they had saved some of their people and they managed to check the disease.

The Twins had been traveling around a lot and had known other people, so at this time they thought they would go and learn whether these other people were sick or not. They went northwest and southeast, all around, and found many people. None had the sickness. Masewi and Oyoyewi were much hated by these other people, who did not know them. So they came back to their people and called a meeting of the Chaianyi, Country Chief, and Antelope Man. They said to the council, "I guess our mother Iatiku does not want us to live here any more." They remembered that Iatiku had told them to go on south to the place known as Haako. "Maybe this sickness is a sign that we should move on." The council decided that it must be so. So Country Chief said he would tell the people they were to leave in 4 days, so they would have time to prepare provisions and make new moccasins and select the things they would need to take with them. He ordered that nothing belonging to the religion (altars, masks, etc.) was to be left behind. All were to help in taking these things along.

When the fourth day came, Country Chief told the chaianyi to go on ahead four lengths (măati'), [149] a long ways, and to prepare a place to stop. So the chaianyi started. They dressed up in their official costumes when they made their first stop.

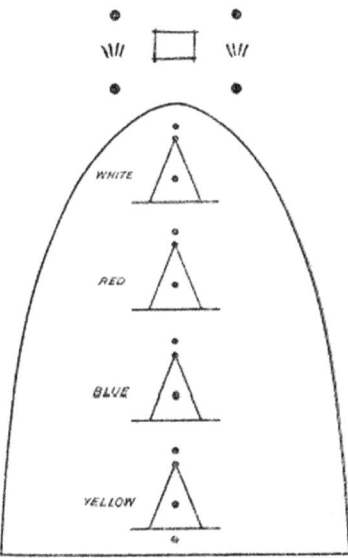

FIGURE 4.--Diagram of rite of exorcism.

They made a sand painting on the south side of the camp, representing four mountains (pl. 15, fig. 1). When the people came, they were to cross these four mountains and valleys and thus put the sickness that much more in their rear. All the people that came walked over, stepping on a mountain and valley in turn. The two chaianyi on the south had their two feathers, and would brush off the sickness of each person as he approached. The chaianyi explained how the people were to stop first halfway on the mountain, then on the top, then in the valley, then halfway up, etc. (fig. 4). The chaianyi would say, as they brushed them off, "Come, Raven! You represent the whirlwind, [150] sweep away from us this disease and all diseases and sadness. You are the one who has the real power to do this." They would repeat this for each person that approached to cross the sand painting. Two chaianyi were at the other end of the sand painting. They were holding two yucca plants cut off at the root and holding them on the ground as though growing. When the person came over the fourth mountain, he would spit his sadness into the middle of the plant. Two other chaianyi were placed at this end where, laid out on the ground, were yucca leaves tied at the four corners (fig. 5). The person steps into the frame. The chaianyi swing it four times backward and spill out his sickness behind him.

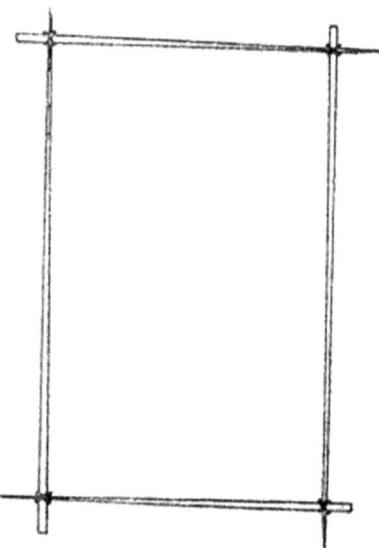

FIGURE 5.--Frame made of yucca plants, used in rite of exorcism.

After passing through the frame, they were told to pass on to a high place where there were two more chaianyi. Before going there they were to pick up any object that caught their eye, any stick or stone, and then to brush themselves with the object they had picked up, speaking to it to take away sickness and sorrow. [151] From there they were allowed to go on. All the people did the same and the chaianyi buried the objects carrying the sickness in the hole that had been dug between them. The medicine men finished their work by destroying the mountains and finally banishing the sickness. Last of all the chaianyi did all of this to each other. Then they made four marks on the ground [152] with an arrowhead, as a barrier to disease, [153] blocking their trail. They traveled for a long time, slowly, as they were on foot and heavily burdened. They came to a place they named Wash'pashŭkă (sage basin). [154] They found water there and the country was beautiful. So Country Chief said to the people, "We will stop here for 4 years and make a pueblo; here we will take along rest." So they made houses with stones and settled down, they built their kivas, carried on their ceremonies, and lived as before.

WANDERINGS, PART XII

WHILE they were living at Washpashuka, the Twins, Masewi and Oyoyewi, traveled around the country a great deal. During their wanderings they found a group of katsina belonging to the Corn clan and these katsina had different names. So when Masewi and Oyoyewi came back and reported that they had found some real katsina, the Corn clan stepped up and said, "They will belong to us, they are our relatives. We will be their friends." So the Corn clan nawai (head man), not knowing how to call these katsina, went to a chaianyi and asked him for advice, should he make an altar for them? Chaianyi said, "Why not? They are real katsina, they have to have an altar." Thus the chaianyi told Corn clan man that he would have to have an altar for himself, for without it he could not call the katsina. So the chaianyi instructed the Corn clan man how to make an altar, and told him to get young sprouts of oak about a year old.

Masewi and Oyoyewi said that these katsina carried canes, so the chaianyi told him to bend these oak sprouts like a cane (crook). The Twins described them and they made several like them. The chaianyi made four honani to be with this altar, but they were to lie flat (as corn is piled) and not set up on end.

One of the katsina always had fire with him. He was called Shura'cha [155] (pl. 1, lower right). He was small and he also had a little canteen, always miraculously full of water. So they thought of calling him to bring some of this water to place in the jar belonging to Antelope Man so the people would never be out of water, and to bring some of his fire, so that they could have him build a fire with it in the center of the plaza, from which the people could all light their hearths and in this way always have fire.

Corn clan man finished his altar and decided to try it out. He asked all of the Corn clan to make prayer sticks and to bring them to the altar. They did as Antelope Man had done, went out and buried the prayer sticks and prayed for the katsina to come. It happened that the katsina received the prayer sticks and the prayer. In the prayer they asked for the water and fire, and the katsina understood. So they knew they were to expect these katsina on the fourth day.

All the Corn clan prepared. They washed their heads so they would look clean and neat. During the 4 days they had purified themselves [by vomiting, probably]. The fourth day was very hot, from early in the morning. Corn clan nawai had told the Corn clan they were to fast on this day. A little after sunrise they saw Shuracha in the distance with smoke around him. He built a series of fires as he approached the pueblo. There were three other katsina with him, Shu'naata, [156] Shumaashka [157] (pl. 7, fig. 2), and Kumootina. [158] The latter was a berdache. [159] They were very slow and took some time to approach. They were not at all lively and poked along. When they came near the pueblo, the Corn clan went out to meet them. Country Chief and his officers acted as guards, keeping other people away. They made a path with corn meal into the plaza. The Corn clan had already built a fireplace in the middle of the plaza and Country Chief had a jar to receive some of the water. Corn clan nawai asked Shuracha to make a fire for them so their people would always have fire, and to put some water in the jar so they would always have water. This katsina was very skillful in making fire and, after the katsina left, the people gathered the fire. The katsina danced four times (the usual ceremony) and about noon they left. (Nowadays at Acoma they bring them into the Corn clan house.)

These katsina dance very slow and sluggishly. They went away like real katsina. These katsina lived west of Washpashuka.

WANDERINGS, PART XIII

THE people lived at Washpashuka a long time. The katsina, used to come and dance for them. After a time, some of the men began to mock the katsina again. They found out who these mockers were; the War chief found out their names. He remembered how the katsina had come and beaten and killed the people when they had mocked them before, so he thought that the best way to punish these people was to dramatize this battle of the katsina. [160] So Country Chief called a council of all the people who knew about the katsina, Antelope Man, and the chaianyi. At this meeting Country Chief told them they were to do this even if it meant the lives of some of their relatives or friends. It took a long time to get the consent of all, as they knew some of the mockers. Even if a man had a son who was a mocker, he had to assist. So they called council after council and picked out the men who were to represent two Gomaiowish messengers, and the man who was to represent Tsitsanits, the leader of the katsina. They decided also to have every member of the Antelope clan, even women and children, to guard against the katsina coming at the people, and they were all furnished with long staffs.

This is what they were to do. Everyone knew the katsina were to regard them [i. e., members of the Antelope clan] as their fathers. So if they held out their staff horizontally in front of a katsina, he should not run over them and not run against the staff. (The katsina must respect this staff. If a katsina touches a staff and another katsina sees him, the second katsina will jump at the first and beat him.) Antelope Man also made an i'chini' [161] (a wall made of skins of buffalo). This was to represent the pueblo. It was understood that the katsina were to whip this ichini and thus symbolically to whip the people. They were not actually to strike the people themselves at all. The ichini was to be set up outside the pueblo where the katsina were to come. (It was set up as a "wall" or "fort" to protect the pueblo.) The katsina were to approach it and strike it with their clubs and weapons.--They took care that those who had mocked the katsina should know nothing of these plans as these mockers were to be killed.

The Corn clan was also asked to call all its members to help at this time. They were to carry the ichini, to set it up, and hold it. The ones who were to impersonate the katsina killed deer [162] and took some of the blood into the kiva and distributed it among the members who were to act as katsina. They filled with blood the intestine of a deer which they were to wear around the neck. (All this was planned in kiva.) The twins Masewi and Oyoyewi were asked to take part. They were to stand on each side of the ichini and when the katsina attempted to strike them, one of the Twins would knock down the katsina and cut the blood-filled intestine on his throat. Antelope Man was to be told, just before the katsina came in, to ask these guilty ones to come with him to the plaza to pray. The katsina were to come. The men [i. e., the mockers], of course, did not know what was to happen. When Antelope Man took them out, the katsina were to spring out and jump on them and catch the guilty ones. They were to chase them around the plaza, catch them, and kill them with clubs. (Originally the real katsina would catch a man and pull him apart; nowadays the impersonators seize him and club him to death.) Then the twins were to come into the plaza and knock down katsina right and left, cutting their "throats."

The ichini was to stand facing west and all the drama was to take place in front of it. The Antelope clan was to stand on each side, winging out from the ichini.

Members of the Katsina society that were to take part in the ceremony went into the mountain, got branches from a hardy oak, made tea, and purified themselves for 4 days. The night of the third day, they made prayer sticks of hard wood.

It was understood that the katsina were to act enraged as they entered the village and were to fight among themselves. If anyone fell or was killed in this fighting, they were not to be brought into the pueblo but were to be buried with their masks on in the wilderness. (This fighting among the katsina as they approach the village is real; they work themselves up into a frenzy. Here grudges and personal disagreements are worked out and several are killed in this fighting. [163] Men who are killed are never mentioned again by anyone. They are just forgotten. In the plaza only the heretics are killed, and while now and then a katsina gratifies a personal grudge against a heretic, these cases are exceptional.)

(Every year, [164] at the season the katsina were killed, katsina are believed to die for three 10's (30 days) and then come to life. At this time the Antelope clan set their altar on the 28th day and say prayers for the Katsina to come alive, and that night they have a dance in kiva.)

When the time came, the men who regarded themselves as manly got together in kiva. It was planned that they should not put on their full costume or make up pretty. (They were to leave off certain feathers from their masks.) They painted their bodies white all over. Early the next morning they went further out into the country and all hid in one place (4 or 5 miles distant from the town). In the pueblo, too, the people were making preparations. They made prayer sticks and painted up, both men and women of the Antelope clan, and put feather down on their heads. They were painted "strawberry" [165] all over but the face. Then the ichini was brought out. The women of Antelope clan were given each a staff (yapi) (pl. 14, fig. 1, c). Masewi blessed the ichini, giving it power. When the time came they also called Shuracha, katsina of the Corn clan.

About noon, two Gomaiowish brought messages to the village from Wenimats. They told Country Chief that the katsina were coming to visit them and bring them gifts and that they would arrive a little after midday. So Antelope Man went and got all the mockers and brought them into his altar and spoke to them and gave them advice.

He showed them how to make prayer sticks with which to pray to the katsina. He told them not to leave there but to wait at the altar and he would lead them out when the katsina came, to pray to them. The Gomaiowish did not accept any of the offerings of Country Chief-tobacco, corn, or meal. They offered them food which they did not accept. They had with them bows and arrows which Country Chief asked for as a gift. They acted like the real Gomaiowish. Antelope chief and the people held them and took away their bows and arrows forcibly. The Gomaiowish then ran away, back to the men who were to impersonate the katsina. The Gomaiowish told them of the incident, exaggerating it, saying they had been almost killed and told them they should fight as hard as they could to kill as many people as they could. So the men put on their masks and started toward the village. There were many of them. On their way they picked up sticks and tore off branches to use as clubs. They selected the strongest they could find. The man acting as Tsitsanits was trying to keep them back.

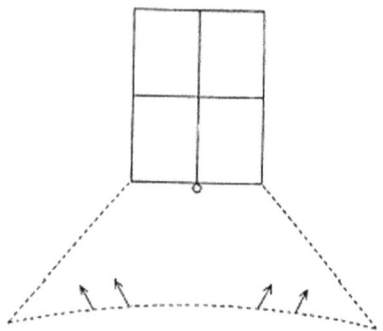

FIGURE 6.--Diagram of ichini and people in front.

The village was all prepared and the ichini was set up in place (fig. 6). The Antelope clan (men, women, and children) were told to stand out in front, holding the staffs to guard the village. (Men and women alternated.) Tsitsanits was ahead and was first to reach the ichini. The men in front lot him through and he leaned against the ichini and rubbed his back against it to gain strength and courage. (Compare pp. 50, 75.)

At first the men were in front. Then, after Tsitsanits came in, they fell back into the "wings," or lines of women. The katsina rushed up to the ichini, striking it four times, then they turned around and ran away. Then anyone could come and strike the ichini; there was a race to see who would be first. The Antelope clan watched to see that no one struck it more than four times. The katsina tried to pass the people but the Antelope clan held their staffs horizontally and barred the way. The ichini was propped up behind by three sticks. As the katsina approached, the Shuracha katsina were behind the ichini (which had been erected by them and the War Twins), When the ichini was set up, the Shuracha started to dance and kept it up during all the time the katsina were striking the ichini, leaving only Masewi and Oyoyewi at the ichini.

After all the katsina had struck the ichini four times, they ran around striking themselves. The Shuracha and the War Twins took down the ichini and carried it into the plaza, where they set it up on the north side. After the ichini was taken down, the line closed in the gap that was left, and the katsina were held back by the Antelope clan.

The mockers were now brought from the altar to the front of the ichini. They did not know there were to be killed. They came out to pray to the katsina and they thought this was to be done in order that they might be forgiven. But the katsina knew what they were to do. When the ichini was moved, the Antelope women were sent ahead with it to form wings and the men held back the katsina. When all was set up, Antelope Man shouted that all was ready. The Antelope Men guarding the katsina turned and ran to the plaza, followed by the katsina; the men took their place in the wings with the women. The katsina rushed in and clubbed to death all the mockers, who were waiting in front of the ichini with their prayer sticks expecting to pray for forgiveness.

Now was the turn of the twins, Masewi and Oyoyewi. They caught the two Gomaiowish and castrated them. The Gomaiowish were the leaders in the killing. They wore their blood bladder in their crotch. Tsitsanits was not killed. He had been stationed well back of the ichini where they could not get at him. Masewi and Oyoyewi then attacked the katsina and cut their throats. Their heads sank down and they fell to earth blood-soaked, simulating death. While lying on the ground they prayed that the blood give new strength to the earth, [166] that the earth produce more.

After Masewi and Oyoyewi had killed all the katsina they took out their staff and arrowhead, the medicine Sun had given them and, going back to the katsina, brought them all back to life. Antelope nawai had prayer sticks with him with which to pray after the katsina had come to life. They prayed that the real katsina would not come again to kill the people. The katsina impersonators acted as if brought to life. This was all dramatization but the guilty ones were really killed, probably 8 or 10. After the Antelope men had made this prayer, the katsina got up and taking the dead mockers with them, left the village. They buried them out in the desert. They did this to make the people believe more strictly in the katsina. The Antelope people then took down the ichini, took it apart, and put it away. The Shuracha, who were dancing all this time, were dismissed and left. [167] --This is the way they passed their time at Washpashuka.

WANDERINGS, PART XIV

A long time passed after this until again they had trouble. Some people did not approve of this dramatization and quarrels started. Some of the relatives of those killed left the tribe. Some of the people said they were not happy at this place, so they decided to leave for the south, remembering that they were to look for Haako further south. So Country Chief notified the people that they were to move, and all was made ready. The people were told to take the masks and altars along and leave nothing sacred behind. So they left with the same ceremonies as before, going on south. It is not known how far they went, but finally they stopped at a place where they went through the ceremony of forgetting. It is not known how far they went when they symbolically crossed the four mountains and left their sickness and trouble behind.

They traveled for many moons and came to a place called Ashthinahawai-sha, Tule Lake. The people were tired and asked if they could not stop there and build another village. So they made camp there, until they finally built better and better houses and forgot about moving on and settled down. Here they lived happily a long time. They had forgotten their quarrels and troubles. Here they had their ceremonies and full village life as before. Many other societies of medicine men were introduced, and there were two or three altars of the Fire Chaianyi and three of the Flint society and three or four more, Giant society altars. (At White House some of the chaianyi had been killed by the katsina; the real katsina did the killing.)

At Tule Lake the people found many ant hills. When they built their houses they destroyed many of the ant homes. The people did not think very much of the ants and they stepped on them and killed them. There came a time when the people become sick with an unknown disease. [168] The sick ones had sores all over their bodies and it seemed as if ants were always running to them as they do to their homes. The medicine men did all they could to cure the people but they failed. In villages which they left behind [? passed by] people had different clan names and one clan was named Ant clan. The chaianyi thought about the Ant clan and decided to make another Society of medicine men. They selected a man to be the first Ant medicine man and gave him an altar; they named him Si·'i chaianyi. He was to have power to cure disease brought on by ants. He had to know the prayers of the ants and how to move them from one place to another, so they would not be destroyed. (There are no Ant chaianyi in Acoma now, [169] but other medicine men have their prayers.) The Ant altar is quite small. There are no sticks. There are one honani and two eagle feathers (the longest on each wing) and the two hands of a horned toad. These were given because the horned toad eats ants. The sand painting represents a horned toad or a lizard (pl. 10, fig. 2, b). A patient is seated on top of the painting. The chaianyi then brushes off the disease with a grass broom. [170] After the patient is brushed off, he is painted with red paint. The gravel [171] that has been swept off the patient is gathered up in a corn husk and buried. Nowadays when a house is being built one of the chaianyi is called to remove the ants. He takes some and the owner digs out the rest. In the tradition it was not necessary for the first Ant chaianyi to do more than brush each patient once to effect a cure. Thus every one got well.

At this time the first chaianyi, the Fire chaianyi, was killed (by the katsina at the katsina war). His altar was lost, as he had plastered it in the wall to hide it. When they moved, his wife located it and brought it along. In the meantime duplicate altars were made at Tule Lake. The people did not know this woman had the original altar in her possession. At Tule Lake there came a famine and the people were starving, there was no rain. Country Chief and Antelope Man tried to bring rain, through the other chaianyi. They failed. So they called a meeting and Country Chief asked if anyone knew where the original altar was. The chaianyi remembered that the altar had disappeared at the time of the katsina attack; they thought that maybe the katsina had stolen it. Masewi and Oyoyewi were at the meeting, and Country Chief asked if they would help seek it. They said, "Yes, we will get it back."

So they went home and put on their magic clothes. They went first to Wenimats. They were gone for many days. They went to the different mountains [of the directions], and they went into the sacred places. They stirred things up in their search. They asked the katsina if they had stolen it. The katsina said no, but the Twins rudely went on searching. In the meantime the woman who had the altar sought Country Chief and brought the altar and asked, "Is this what you have lost?"

WANDERINGS, PART XV

IN the meantime the Twins had made the katsina angry. They called a meeting of the katsina from all directions to meet at North Mountain to discuss what to do about the Twins who had been so rude and who had so much power against them. The officers of each of the four directions (the rain makers) were at the meeting. They had been holding this council many days and were tired. The Twins came in at this time and found the katsina asleep. Shakak on the north side had there the staff with which he made snow. This they stole. On the west Morityema had the staff with which he made hail. This they stole. On the south side Maiyochina had the staff with which he made lightning and the balls with which thunder is made. They stole them. in the east Shruisthia had the staff with which he made frost. They took it, too.

In the meantime the people had set up the missing altar of the Fire society. Fire chaianyi spoke to the honani as though it were Iatiku. "You have promised us a happy life, but we are in need of water. See if you can give us all the water that you have." The chaianyi made a mistake there. The people did not know why they asked for so much water.

After the Twins stole these staves they said to the katsina, "Go on sleeping. We have everything with which you work and we can use them as well as you. We will do so. We are going to take them and plant them in the ground and we challenge you to dig them up. If you can do that, we will believe in you." This was also a mistake on the part of the Twins. They had made the katsina angry.

On their way back the Twins buried the staves but did not bury them deeply. The katsina awoke and heard all they had said, but they could do nothing as the Twins had run off. So the katsina had another meeting. They were at a loss as to how to get the best of the Twins. But they thought of bringing to life Tsits shuwi (water snake), so named because it travels like a stream of water. They told it to chase the Twins and devour them. The katsina said also, "Let us go! We are going to take our staves away from the Twins."

The Twins did not get far from where they had buried the staves before a large cloud appeared that was followed by a cloudburst. Lightning tried to strike them, but they shielded themselves with the buckskin shirts their father had given them. The flints [172] stuck in the buckskin and the Twins jerked them on through and breathed power from them, saying, "Thank you! With this I will be more manly." They traveled back toward the village and all the way it was raining. When they reached the village they found the lake had overflowed and driven out the people. Many people had been struck by lightning and killed. When they returned, they stretched their buckskins so as to shield all the people, so no more were struck. So the spirits who rule in the four directions said, "We give up. I guess we cannot kill them." But they let the snake follow their instructions.

It continued to rain. The people were completely driven from their homes and were able to take with them only the altars and the things they needed most. The people moved on south to a high mountain, All the chaianyi worked, [173] and Country Chief and Antelope Man prayed for it to stop raining. But no one listened to them There were many animals driven to this mountain and many different peoples (maybe the people who had separated at kashkach, White House), Some spoke different languages, others spoke similarly. All were shielded under the buckskin. The world began to fill with water and the dashing waves almost swept them from the mountain. So the Twins, seeing the large waves, said, "That must be Water Snake, He is coming to kill us." They had never used the four arrows their father had given them and they said, "Perhaps this is where we are to use these arrows." So they watched carefully until they saw the biggest wave coming up. They said, "This is where his heart is." Each shot an arrow into it. After they had done this the waves came slower and became a huge snake which wrapped itself around the mountain where the Twins killed it, using up the rest of the arrows, each shooting four times. So everything became calm and there was no more rain. The water started to recede, but very slowly. It is said that formerly the mountains were beautifully smooth and rounded. But this flood and the receding waters cut canyons and gullies and made it rough.

It is not known how long they camped on this mountain, but they always had food, and the animals that had been saved were increasing, When things began to get dry, they all separated again, not being able to understand each other.

WANDERINGS, PART XVI

THE people were still looking for Haako. They had not lost the two eggs that had been given them. They said, "This cannot yet be the right place, our bad luck shows that." So they got out into the plains again and moved south. They passed many ruins where people had been living before and they crossed the paths of other people. These people were enemies of each other. It is not known how these others had been saved from the flood. When attacked by enemies, the Twins would go out alone to fight, and they always won by virtue of their father's power. They thought they would keep track of how many they killed. So after killing an enemy, they would put their thumb on the head and scalp it, cutting around the thumb.

They traveled on and passed a place called Kawaíka [174] (lake), where Laguna stands. Here they stopped for the forgetting ceremonies. [175] There was no town here at that time. South of the lake they symbolically crossed the four mountains. When they got to a place which they called Kutsekatsa (place of antelope; antelope range), because there were very many antelope there--when they got there they asked if they could rest, as they had seen many antelope and they said it would be a good place to stop. They camped there and found water. The name of the place was Shuimi kaiya (turquoise cave). There is a big rock about 10 miles northeast of Acoma of white sandstone; on the north side is a cave with water coming from it. While they camped here they had good luck killing antelope. They traveled around the region and found a place called Dyaptsiam [176] (dyap, a hardwood tree; tsiam, pass or gap). The people thought of moving there to build another village. Some of them said it must be Haako, as they found turkeys and antelope in plenty. So they broke camp and at Dyaptsiam built a new village.

Here they again established their altars and ceremonies. The chaianyi cleared the place of diseases. The chaianyi always took a basket of prayer sticks which they buried in the center of the proposed site, and under the basket they buried an arrowhead. This was to protect the pueblo. Some of the people wanted to live at the bottom of the mesa, but the Twins said that it would be better to live on top, where they could look around, and when they left it they could look back and see their home outstanding and think of it as a wonderful place. Also it would furnish them protection. Some others did not agree that that was the right place, so they broke away from those who agreed with the Twins, saying, "We have seen another mesa that is more imposing, we will build our home there." This was further south. This was called Katsima (braced cliff, [177] talus cliff, the Enchanted Mesa). A few families, very few, went up but they soon ran out of water and after a time rejoined those at the other village. They built a pretty village on the low mesa, Dyaptsiam. (The ruins are still there.)

Here they lived a long time contentedly because there was much game. Here they found many turkeys. They had many ceremonies every season and got along well. They had with them masks representing Chakoya katsina. No one had ever used them. It was a different kind of mask covering only the face. They know that these Chakoya were very good hunters and fond of game. So it came to their mind that they had these masks and they recalled they were good hunters. Since they had no such game, they thought of calling them and bringing them to dance. All agreed that it would be good, so more of the masks were made. The men belonging to the katsina [organization] met in kiva. Country Chief brought the masks to the chaianyi to be brought to life, with the usual ceremony. The men who were going to take part went through the ceremony and went out into the country and put on their masks and costumes. The people were expecting the Chakoya, so the impersonators visited the village, The people found that these Chakoya had very pretty songs in a language easy to understand. Their songs always named game and told how to hunt. The first time they were called it was near spring time and they had plenty of snow, and they were lucky in their hunting. They found the Chakoya dance to be pleasant and interesting because it was new. When the dancers finished, the people went home and the dancers went into the country to decostume. This was a secret dance and they did not let the people know that they were not real.

It was time for planting. Antelope Man recalled that Iatiku had told him the people were to have a dance every season before planting time, so he told Country Chief to wait and not plant yet; they were going to have a dance to make all kinds of crops. All the people were told to meet in kiva where Antelope man was to tell them how to dance and for what reason. This they did and Antelope Man told them that mother Iatiku advised them to dance this Auwĕ before planting. So he told them to make images of corn, pumpkins, and beans, and bring them on the night that they were to gather to dance, These songs and dances had been taught them by Iatiku in Shipapu but they had forgotten them.

Antelope Man set up his altar in kiva. The people came to the dance and brought their images, which they placed in front of the altar. They recalled some of the songs and they had a dance. This dance lasted all night. The men would dance in a circle (inside kiva) for a while, then they would rest and the women would dance. [178] This continued till nearly sunrise. Then Antelope Man told them to come forward to the altar and get the images they had brought. He told them that their prayers in the dances were now with these images. They were to take these and again pray to the directions, then they were to take the images to the gardens and plant them. This was done and they found that it was good. They had abundant harvests,

The twins Masewi and Oyoyewi were very helpful to the people, They were always up early [179] and they went out into the country and yelled to the clouds (katsina). It is not known how long they lived at this place. The Twins were always traveling. One time they went to South Mountain, the home of Maiyochina, the Summer ruler, who is the spirit of the south direction. When the Twins got there they found that Maiyochina had a guard who was not to let anyone in. They asked him his name and he told them Gaukapuchume [180] (busybody? someone always wanting to do something). The Twins found him to be very skillful, a good gambler, a good stick runner, and quick witted. He challenged the Twins to different games and taught them a new game; how to win arrows from each other. They had won a lot of his property. They put up a target. Whoever got closest to it would win. (Gaukapuchume wanted to get the sacred arrows, which he knew they had.)

They had a race on which they bet arrows. The guard was old and lost, so the Twins won everything he had to bet. The old man got angry. He still had a baby's head made up to look like a ball. It was full of blood. They did not want to gamble for this yet, so they asked him where Haako was, they had come to ask Maiyochina, but since they had not yet seen Maiyochina they would ask the guard. So he answered, "'Maybe you know the place Katsima. Haako is just southwest of that place, a large rock. You will find it by going to the northeast end and yelling. Then you will hear the echo very distinctly. This is the place you are looking for." He asked the Twins to give him back what they had won in return for this information. But the Twins would not do so, saying, "You were the one who started betting and you taught us how to gamble. You lost, so the winnings are ours." Gaukapuchume asked them once more to give them back, and the Twins said no. He asked a third time with the same result. He asked the fourth time. Still they refused. Then the old man hit the ball with a stick up against the wall of the house. It splattered blood and, on falling to the floor, started to cry like a baby. This frightened the Twins and they ran out, taking their winnings with them. The old man chased them hitting toward them the ball, which always cried. Piece by piece, Masewi and Oyoyewi dropped the things they had won as they fled. After getting away from Gaukapuchume, they stopped to talk it over, saying, "This is the first time I have ever been frightened; were you frightened, too? He must have supernatural power." But they did not think much about it, and returned to their home.

Upon returning, they stayed a long time, but one day they went to Country Chief and told him what they had learned. They told him that it was that place farther south that was the real Haako and they left it up to him to find out. He was the one to look for it and see if the echo was there. So Country Chief called the chaianyi to a meeting and told them the message Masewi and Oyoyewi had brought back from South Mountain. He told the chaianyi also that he still had the two eggs which Iatiku had given them to bring to Haako. "We should not stay here longer," he said. "I will go on ahead and find if it is the right place." So they set a date for him to leave with some of the chaianyi. The chaianyi invited Masewi and Oyoyewi to come along, So they went to the south to look for Haako.

They saw this rock and went toward the northeast end. Country Chief cried out, "Haako!" and they all listened. He yelled four times to make sure, and every time the echo came back clearly. They all agreed this must be the place. They returned to the people and had another meeting. They recalled that they had been instructed to break the parrot egg at Haako and they were to take the crow's egg on afterward to Kuyapukauwak. They decided to move, as the distance was not far and they had been told by Iatiku to go to this place. Country Chief told all the people to prepare for 4 days and to move. He told them to get everything ready so as to leave nothing behind. The people were glad they were near Haako and were anxious to move.

On the fourth day they left, and on the same day reached the foot of the rock. They gathered close around Country Chief who held up the two eggs, telling them, "These were given us by Iatiku. One is a parrot egg. The other is a crow egg. You are to choose the egg you think is the parrot egg." He told them to step up one at a time. He placed the two eggs on a piece of buckskin and told each person to stand on the side they chose as the one which was the parrot egg. (The one to choose was the head of the family, the father). [181] The chaianyi were the first to make their choice, then came the people. After this was done there was a woman just about to bear a child. She said, "When my baby comes she will belong to the Parrot clan."

Country Chief picked up the egg the Twins had chosen, and said, "This will be the parrot egg [?]. Those who have chosen this egg will live here, at Haako." He told them they must not retract their choice, but must stay on the side they had chosen. He told them the parrot was supposed to be a very pretty bird and would be useful, while the crow would be a pest and good for nothing. Most of the chaianyi and Country Chief himself were on the side of the egg he was going to break. He stepped back, telling the people to watch very carefully. This egg was blue and was very pretty, while the other was a dull color. He started to count, one, two, three, four. On the fourth count he threw it against the rock. When it hit it broke and a number of crows flew out of it. The losers felt badly, [182] but they could not retract, because Iatiku had told them if they did so they would never live happily there [?anywhere]. Country Chief told them, "This ends our journey, The rest must journey on to Kuyapukauwak and take the other egg with them."

They all camped at this place. There were some chaianyi who were with those who were to go on south. They were given their altars and some of the masks to take with them. Most of the officers were to remain, so they had to make new officers for the other group. They were to make a new Country Chief, so the old Country Chief chose a man and instructed him in his duties, giving him duplicates of the necessary things. Antelope Man did the same, appointing a man to take his place with the other group. When the time came to separate, a meeting was held and Country Chief and Antelope Man told the departing people who their officers were to be. This was a very sad time for both groups. The parrot group then left toward the south and it is not known how far they went.

The people who remained were told by Country Chief to build a village at the foot of this rock. They did this and it is not known how long they lived in this village. They carried on their ceremonies as before. They were lucky and happy because they had come to their permanent home.

WANDERINGS, PART XVII

MASEWI and Oyoyewi were active as usual, traveling in different countries, from which they brought back many scalps of people they killed. The rulers in the four directions did not like the Twins, so they held a meeting and decided that the Twins were doing too much wrong, that they were afraid of nothing nor anybody. They decided the Twins should be punished. [183] So they called Pishuni hachtsa [old man] (the evil spirit) to help them. When he came they asked him if he would help them punish the Twins, and told him the wrongs they had been doing. So he said, "Yes, I'll be glad to help. Leave it all to me. I will find a way to punish them."

Pishuni watched the village at Haako for someone to die. The Twins had known a girl at the village who was a very good character. Pishuni worked on this girl, causing her to die. So at the time of her death he went into her house and painted himself with some of this girl's blood, assuming the likeness of the girl. He met the Twins and spoke to them. The girl was very attractive and the Twins liked her and invited her to their home. She told the Twins she loved them and would like to live with them in their home. So they told their mother that this girl wanted to live with them, and the mother was pleased. They let the girl stay and at night she crept in between the Twins as they slept, but they did not know it. (Before they went to sleep she had crawled in with them, but they turned over and slept.)

While Masewi and Oyoyewi slept the girl turned into a corpse of horrible appearance. She fondled one of them and he awoke to see her as an emaciated, naked bag. He then got up, crying to his brother, "Look, someone has lain down with us." But before the other spoke the girl Pishuna, spoke, saying, "It is I, you are my husband, don't you remember you invited me to live here?" and tried to pull them back. The Twins were frightened and ran out of the house followed by Pishuna. The spirit was called Ko'oko, a haunt. Thus, if a man murders another, he is always haunted by Kooko at night. [184]

She followed the Twins all night. They would go a distance and try to rest, but she would catch up and speak to them. She kept haunting them in this manner for many days and nights. They thought of running to North Mountain to try to get help. They went into the home of the ruler of the North, Shakak, telling him that they were being followed by this woman and that they came to ask help. Shakak said, "Yes, I will help you." So they rested a while, but it was not long before Pishuna was near by yelling for the Twins: "Are my husbands there?" Shakak had known that the evil spirit was to punish the Twins, so he answered, "Yes, they are here, come down and get them!" Pishuna came down and started again to speak to the Twins. She asked why they were running away, coaxing them to come to her.

The Twins ran out and Pishuna followed close at their heels. They tried to rest, but Pishuna was always waking them up. They ran until they went to Wenimats for help. They went into the kiva of Tsitsanits and asked for help. He also knew that they were being punished, but he consented to lot them rest. When Pishuna came, though, he let her in to them. Tsitsanits made the excuse of saying they had better leave because she was so ugly looking. He could give them a place to sleep but nothing else. So they left and Pishuna after them.

Next they ran to West Mountain, for help. They had not eaten since they left home. They were hungry and tired. They asked Morityem for help, and he consented to help them. He asked them what was wrong with the bows and arrows they had used so successfully for killing people. They said they could not use them any more as they were too frightened to shoot straight. So Morityem said he would help, that it could not be anybody very fierce to scare these Twins. He also knew that the Twins must be punished, so he let Pishuna in when she called. He let her in, telling her, "Take your husbands out, you are so ugly I can't do anything with you."

So the Twins ran, heading for Gaukapuchume, the gambler of South Mountain. They were exhausted by now and Pishuna was just about to get them, as they were about to give up. They rushed into the house of Gaukapuchume and frightened him. They told him not to fear, that they were being chased and they had come to him for help. Gaukapuchume was flattered that two such brave men should come to him for help, so he said, "Yes, I'll help you. What's wrong that you are not manly any more?" He told them to take a rest. He took his ball (the baby head) and his stick and when

Pishuna yelled asking for the Twins, he replied, "Yes, they are here, come on in!" He had his ball and stick ready. He hit the ball toward Pishuna. The ball struck her on the chest. It splashed blood and Pishuna was frightened and turned and fled. The ball cried at the same time. Gaukapuchume followed with his stick, striking the ball toward Pishuna. He was a good runner and chased the evil spirit, hitting the ball four times, and following after each stroke. On the fourth hit, the ball chased the evil spirit into pishuni ha'ach, home of the evil spirit. He turned back, letting the ball chase Pishuna.

He returned to the Twins, who were almost dead with exhaustion. He made fun of them, saying, "It is not true after all that you are brave. I have won from you the title of bravery. I am going to tell you why you have been punished. You have been killing people all over the country and have left their bodies scattered all over. That is the reason this Kooko was chasing you. From now on do not kill just for the purpose of sport and just because you think you are brave. Human beings are sacred (precious). They are not like animals. Unless you know how many scalps you have taken, I am going to send you back to your people. When you get there you are to take your scalps and wash them. You are also to dance for the public. But from the day you wash the scalps, you are to fast 30 days (and observe continence). After the thirtieth day you are to come out and dance." They were to call the Koshari (impersonators) to be the leaders in this dance. [185] He taught them how to dance and how to carry the scalps. They were to have cedar branches, one scalp to hang from each twig. They were to get a long pole to the top of which they would tie the scalps. They were to place this pole in the plaza 4 days before they danced. On the fourth day they were to come out and dance all day, and at sundown after finishing the dance they were to take down the pole. Then for 30 days more they were to remain continent. He told them, "If you do not keep this fast the Kooko will come to haunt you again." He told them that the scalps should not be thrown away. After the dance they were to belong to the tribe. After these instructions were given them, they left and returned to the village.

When they returned to the village, the people noticed that they seemed very sad and run down physically. As soon as Country Chief heard about them, he came to see them. He asked them why they were in that condition. They answered, "Yes, I guess we do look that way. We will not tell you just now, but will tell you tonight. Go and call the people to meeting. Have all of the chaianyi and officers present." So Country Chief went up the streets crying out and telling the people. Iit the evening at the appointed time they met in kiva. Country Chief went after the Twins. When they came to the meeting they were not smiling and looking happy and alert and lively as usual. They seemed to have lost their aggressiveness. There were whispers going around, "Why do they look like this? Someone must have beaten them."

Country Chief gave the Twins cigarettes to smoke. (The Indians always use this tobacco when they are going to ask an important question or a favor from anyone). The Country Chief offered it to them telling them to rest and smoke, then to tell why they had wished the meeting called. After they had smoked, Masewi, the elder, rose and spoke, "Yes, it is true, I know you are talking to us. It is true that we have made a mistake. You have always known us to be superior. We have never told you, but we have killed many people in our travels and their bodies are scattered all around. For this reason punishment was brought upon us by the Skau'pistaia. [186] For this reason they brought alive Kooko for us. They almost got the best of us with the Kooko. But Gaukapuchume helped us conquer it. We were saved in the South Mountain. For 8 days and 8 nights we were without sleep, food, or water. We were chased to South Mountain. But we were saved and we have brought back instructions from Gaukapuchume which are to be followed always from now on. He told us that we two were to dance with the scalps of the people we have killed. But first we are to set a date from which we are to purify ourselves and confess with prayers to latiku, whose people we have destroyed. But we will tell you and you will see how we go through this ceremony and you will watch and listen and learn every step of it. We will ask Country Chief to ask the Koshari to be with us in this ceremony, which they will rule. This is the reason we wished this meeting called. I hope we have not caused you too much bother. You will hear of the date that we will set at another time." The meeting adjourned and the people started talking, saying it was true the Twins had been too impetuous and forward.

The Twins returned to their home and told their mother she was to be womanly and was to help them with what they had to go through, and they said a prayer to her. They told her she was to take part in the dance with them. They knew she had the hardest part to do, for she had to dance all day long. They set the next day to start their fast. Though they were still sick and tired, they went out and got twigs to make their prayer sticks. For 4 days they worked making them and putting them in baskets until four baskets were filled. They made a new costume for themselves. They strung bear claws for a necklace and they made clothing of skins of game animals with a shoulder girdle [bandoleer] of the skin of beasts of prey. To this a pouch was attached. In it was gravel obtained from ant hills. The flint arrowheads which they had pulled through the skin when they had been chased by Lightning at Tule Lake were sewed to the outside. Tassels hanging from the pouch were each of different kinds of skins. All parts of it were taken from enemies they had killed.

After the twelfth day, they called Country Chief to tell him to tell his people they should make songs to be used in dramatizing the bringing of scalps into the pueblo. (They were to act as though they had killed an enemy and were bringing in the scalp.) [187] Country Chief did as he was asked to do. The men gathered and made songs. They had a song they were to use when the scalps were to be brought in and to sing to them all night till sunrise.

On the eighth day at midnight, Masewi and Oyoyewi took the scalps and went out into the country. They went quite a distance from the village. They stopped at an ant hill and broke it up, putting the scalps on it. They made a miniature house (hogan) over the scalps. They asked the ants to "whip" the scalps and to "kill" and "eat" them. The ants did so. The Twins gave their war cry while jumping back and forth over the pile. They had brought with them one of the baskets of prayer sticks and with them they prayed to the north. They buried the prayer sticks, leaving the scalps. The next night they went to the west with another basket of prayer sticks; then they returned and rested. The next night they wept to the South and did likewise and on the fourth night to the east and did the same.

The fourth time they did not return but went on to where they had left the scalps. They had told Country Chief they would announce their coming by giving their war cry. So they cried out when they came near the village, and the people heard them. Country Chief heard them also, so he likewise cried out for all the able-bodied men to come out into the plaza. Giving the war cry, Masewi and Oyoyewi approached as the people gathered in the plaza. Country Chief was coaxing the people to hurry; they were frightened. The Twins finally came into the crowd and they told the people, "The Moishumoi [188] (enemies) are coming after us; we have killed some of them."

They told all the able-bodied men to get their weapons and bring a little lunch. Most of the men rushed back to their houses to get weapons and food. This was the first time they were going on the war path and the women were encouraging the men. Every man was out, none stayed behind. Masewi and Oyoyewi led the attack.

When they arrived at the place where the scalps were, the Twins said, "Here is the place," and they started to shoot arrows and throw their clubs at the scalps. After everyone had done this, the Twills gave orders to stop and they told the people that they were now going to "take a scalp." They told the people to watch closely to see how it was done. They would rush up to the hogan, acting as though they were fighting and cutting the scalp from an enemy. They would take one scalp after another and throw it over their shoulder. After they had gathered them all up, they told the people to get shoots of young cedar and cut down a 12-foot pole. The cedar shoots were tied to the top of the pole and from each twig a scalp was tied. After this was done they told the people, "We are going to take the scalps back to the village and we are going to sing the first song." As they came toward the village they sang (there are about 20 songs used), Masewi carried the pole, no one else could touch it. If anyone touched it, he would be haunted by Kooko.

When they were near the village, all the women gathered around them. The pole was planted in the middle of the plaza. Then Masewi said, "Four days from now my brother and I will dance. But I ask all of you people to help with our dance. For 4 days you will practice this dance. Our mother is going to do the ashia (the name of her part in the dance)." He told the people, "This is the way you are to pay tribute to your warriors if they conquer some other people." [189]

That same night Country Chief had asked that the Koshari come out of the kiva. They were to go from house to house and gel, the people to go to the kiva to practice. Masewi told the people they were to regard the Koshari as rulers during these 4 days; they were to rank above Country Chief, Antelope Man, and all the chaianyi. He said that the people were not to have cigarettes unless they asked the Koshari to make them for them. (We make this rule very strict. If anyone smokes a cigarette he makes himself during these 4 days, he would be haunted by the scalps, or would be the first to be killed or injured in battle.)

Every evening at sundown during these 4 days Koshari would gather the people and bring them to the kiva where Masewi and Oyoyewi were. They helped with the songs and encouraged the people to be brave and patient. During these 4 days the Twins were fixing up the costumes they were to wear in the dance. It was the first time the people would see them in the costume their father had given them, and how they were painted.

The night before the dance they took their mother into the kiva to practice her dance. They made different headdresses for her to wear. That night the Koshari told the people they were all to be in the kiva before sunrise. Just about daybreak the Koshari came out of the kiva and got on the housetop and sang a song. All were in their Koshari costume. Early in the morning they went from house to house telling people to come to kiva. The Twins had asked two chaianyi to help dress them in kiva. They were supposed to be resting and not to help themselves, but they instructed the chaianyi how to paint them and in what they wanted to wear.

As soon as the sun came up, the Koshari said the dance was to start. All the people came out and took position on the plaza.

The mother [190] of the twins goes in dancing among the men as they come into the plaza. When the song is over the men stop, and the mother dances alone back of the pole, Masewi and a chaianyi sitting between her and the pole. She dances just one song by the pole, then they all go back to kiva, where they rehearse more songs. In the first dance Masewi, the elder twin, comes out; in the second dance Oyoyewi, the Younger twin, comes out.

The Twins had asked some women to prepare food at their home for all the people. They always had plenty of meat, being great hunters. This was the first time the people were to hold a feast all together. At noon the Koshari told the people that the women were to bring food and gather at the kiva. They had a big feast, some ate outside and others in kiva. The Koshari told the people after they had eaten they were to continue the dance in the afternoon until sundown.

When the dance was over, the Twins said a prayer for the people and thanked them for taking part in the ceremony. The people then left and rested. The Twins took down the pole and told the people that the scalps belonged to the tribe, and anyone wishing to be brave might come and ask the scalps for power. [191] They told the people that they were to go through this ceremony any time that an enemy was killed. This dance is also to pay respect to the enemy who has been killed, so he will not haunt the killer.

So they took the scalps off the pole and took them back to their home. At their home they built an addition especially for the scalps to live in. For 30 days more they were to purge themselves and remain continent. After these 30 days they would be free of Kooko and would not be haunted. This is the end of the ceremony. (One who kills an enemy is known as Opi or Masewi, he always represents Masewi. The last of these, an old man, about 25 years ago, had the scalps buried, there would be no one to feed them and care for them when he died, and he feared sickness or pests might come to the village as a result.) [192]

From this day on, the Twins were much more careful of what they did and were not so impetuous and purposeless in their activities. Every time a man killed an enemy, they held this ceremony and they got their instructions from the Twins how to go about it. The Twins said that they were not very happy any more and that they were no longer fit to be with the people and that they were going to disappear. They said that they were going to take their mother and the three would go on top of the east point of the rock [193] (at Acoma). They said they selected this place because they knew that Iatiku meant for the people to live on top of the rock, as it would be more wonderful and mysterious. [194] "So we are going ahead in order to disappear there." Shortly after this Masewi, Oyoyewi, and their mother were missed by the people.

WANDERINGS, PART XVIII

IT is not known how much longer the people lived at the bottom of the rock, but much time elapsed. Many officers died away but finally there came a time when Kasewat [195] was Country Chief, being the only son of the war chief [?]. The older people remembered that Kasewat had said that eventually they were to move on top of the rock and in that way they would also be protected, for the people were the "chosen people." So they decided to carry out the plan of Kasewat. There were still many pine trees on top of the mesa. The chaianyi went ahead and planted their prayer sticks on the site. Country Chief asked the men to go up and clear off the site and level it. He asked them to make a trail up to the top on the south side. They called it the rainbow ladder (fig. 1, 2, pp. 23, 24). The chaianyi were asked to bring down all the ants. They moved down all the other living things, like centipedes and snakes, that were not wanted there.

Kasewat made a duplicate of his broken prayer stick and buried it where the plaza was to be. Then he asked the chaianyi to make four lengths of prayer sticks [? road prayer feathers], which would make a trail to the center of the plaza. The Antelope clan made their prayer stick [feathered string] to lead to where their headquarters were to be. The rest of the chaianyi did likewise, planting their prayer sticks at the places where their kivas were to be. Country Chief did the same for all the public kivas and for his headquarters.

When all was ready, Country Chief and the Antelope clan were the first to be helped in building their houses. Everyone was to help.

After finishing one place, Country Chief would say what clan would come next. They helped each other thus. But before they had finished all the buildings, the water ran out. So they cleaned out the hollow places in the rock for cisterns [196] and walled in some so that they would hold more. When the next rain came they had plenty of water. They built the home [?house ?houses] for the Antelope clan. After all the houses had been built, Country Chief told the people it was time for them to move up on Yakakotona kanach [197] (completely kernelled long ear of corn).

So the chaianyi were the first to go up the Rainbow trail. The chaianyi brushed the disease from the people before they climbed up. They were to help the people up. The chaianyi were to go up first and the people below were to ask permission to come up on Yakakotona. Country Chief came first to the bottom of the trail and asked permission: "Dini (up on top!), Country Chief asks if he will be allowed to come up." The chaianyi answer, "Yes, come on up, bring all your game, all your beads, all your crops. Bring long life and leave nothing behind. Come up!" The chaianyi had made different places along the trail where they were to go and pray. One chaianyi was along to instruct the people as they came. The first place was where the lion was to guard, next was where the bear was to guard. The next above, the frog (green) was to guard. The last, near the top, the snake was to guard. Country Chief prayed at each of these places, then the chaianyi let him pass.

The Antelope clan was next and then the rest came in turn in the same manner. When Country Chief had come up, he was formally directed to his house and then the rest were directed in the same manner, by the chaianyi, to their houses. It took 2 days to move all the people up, for every ceremonial detail was observed for each clan and society. After the people were moved, the chaianyi were asked by Country Chief to initiate [?] the kivas and to put guards on each of the four walls. After all was completed they lived for a long time there, year after year going through their ceremonies. This is as far as the tradition is told.

The tradition is told and taught when a man is being initiated into the of the societies. During the 4-day period while the chaianyi are letting up the altar, they tell it. The songs contain information also. Besides, in preparing for a ceremony, that part of the tradition which may relate to it is told. Before the Kopishtaiya come, for example, when the men are getting ready for them, they tell in kiva the part they are going to enact. Thus they will be thoroughly familiar with the spirit and details of the ceremony.

THE BIRTH OF THE WAR TWINS

AFTER the famine at White House there was a woman living with her daughter. This girl and her mother were hated by everyone. They took care of their own field and no one spoke to them or invited them to their house. But the katsina were very fond of them, as they always made offerings to them.

It was customary for the people to go out to pick prickly pears, piñons, and yucca fruit. One season there was plenty of piñons so the daughter asked her mother if she could go and gather some, but her mother said, "There is no one to take care of you." The girl insisted, saying she could go alone. So she took a lunch and followed the other people. She came to where the people were camped; no one invited her in, so she camped alone. She passed the night and the next day went out picking piñons all alone. At noon suddenly someone met her. He was Oshach Paiyatiuma, Sun Youth, [198] spirit and ruler of the Sun (pl. 1, center left). He spoke to the girl saying, "Are you picking piñons?" (Such greeting is applied to what anyone is doing.) "Yes," she said, "but you frightened me." Sun said, "I will help you pick piñons, but I have brought you two piñons; I want you to eat them." She asked who he was. He told her, "I am Sun." She asked where he lived. He said, "Hakuoikuchaha (where the sun rises)." She thanked him for the piñons.

She ate the piñons after he left, and became pregnant. He had promised to help her pick piñons, so whenever she picked piñons they increased in her basket. Seeing that she had more than she could carry, she decided to return home. So she put the load on her back, but it was not heavy. When she got home her mother praised her, saying, "You have certainly gathered lots of piñons." They noticed the others drying piñons on the roofs of houses, so they did the same. When they spilled out the piñons they grew into a large pile. The mother and the girl were astonished to see how many she had brought. The girl told her mother how Sun Youth had promised aid. She also said that he had given her two piñons to eat and maybe that explained what had happened. She did not know that she was to have children from these piñons.

Time passed and her pregnancy became noticeable. Her mother noticed it and asked if she were pregnant. She said, no, for she knew she had met no man. The other people noticed her condition too and said she was pregnant. Soon she gave birth to two children. After 4 days they were presented to the Sun and given names. Their names were: Masewi (the elder) and Oyoyewi (the younger). She wondered how she had gotten that way and then she remembered eating the two piñons of Sun Youth.

The babies were very small and did not look handsome, but they grew rapidly. They were soon crawling and before long began to walk. They started to speak very early. They began leaving the house and were not afraid to go out. Their grandmother cautioned them not to go too far from the village as the animals would get them, but they paid little attention. They grew very fond of hunting, starting with birds and rabbits, and when they came home they would speak of the animals they had seen. They spoke of seeing an animal with horns (rabbit) and asked grandmother if it was something to eat. Their grandmother told them it was a rabbit, so they asked how to kill it. They would wander off, remaining all day away. So their grandmother said, "I'll make you something to kill it with." She had an old basket she was no longer using. She took the circular stick forming the rim of the basket and cut it in two. She tied sinew connecting each end of the two segments. Giving one of these bows to each boy she said, this is ostiaha, "bow." (She got the word from the rainbow.) [199]

The grandmother got some stirring sticks from a bundle for stirring corn. She took two of these sticks, giving one to each boy, saying, "You are to use this with the bow. These are istoa, "arrows." She showed them how to use it. (They had said they had tried to catch the rabbit but it was too fast.)

Then they went out with their new weapons to hunt. Their father, the Sun, was always watching them and helped them. It was he who made them grow fast and mature quickly. So he watched to see how they would use the bow and arrow. When they saw a rabbit they crawled up to it and shot at it. The arrow just touched the rabbit, but the rabbit fell. They ran up and caught the rabbit. It was by the power of the Sun that they had done this. [200] They took it home and their grandmother and mother were much pleased. They were so pleased with their success they were anxious to do more hunting. Sometimes they played with other children, but they were mean to the other children and being stronger made them cry. However, they preferred to go alone to the country to hunt. With the help of the Sun they began to kill larger game. They easily found deer and antelope which the Sun made come to them.

Any large animal they killed was too heavy to carry, so they would come back for their grandmother. She taught them to skin game with obsidian. Grandmother feared they would wander too far, so she tried to scare them by telling them the lions and bears, [201] would take them off. Instead of being scared, each time she would name a new fierce animal, they would go out and look for it, after she described it for them. They kept their grandmother very busy making buckskin. Soon they began killing large animals like lions and bears and kept their grandmother busy making rugs. Once their grandmother told them the bear would eat them, so they went out to find the bear and see if it was true a bear would try to eat them. They invented a stick with which to fight if the bear should prove dangerous. They got a stick of hard wood about 9 inches long and sharpened at both ends, saying, "With this we will overpower you." They came to two cubs, so they started to play with them, running them around till the cubs whined and cried as the boys teased them, poking sticks in their eyes. But the boys kept watch for the mother. Soon they heard her coming. The bear charged at them, but they stood their ground. Masewi was in front and poked the two-pointed stick in the bear's mouth as it bit at him. The bear stopped and started to paw at its mouth while the boys stood by and laughed. It was great fun for them. After they had laughed as much as they wanted, they killed the bear. They had learned from their grandmother that the chaianyi used bear paws, so they thought they would take them off as presents for the chaianyi. [202] (This is what Koshari would have done, as paws for chaianyi may not be taken this way.)

After they grew a little older they heard other children speak of their fathers. So they went to their mother and asked her why they did not have someone to know as father, like the other children. So their mother told them their father did not live there. The boys asked where he lived and the mother told them at Hakuoikuchaha. They asked how far it was to that place and how many times the sun would come up before they could reach it. Their mother said she did not know, that it was where the sun came up. The boys asked their mother if they could go to visit their father. She told them they could never get there and it was no use trying. She did not think they would try. They had always gotten up early before sunrise. They always prayed early in the morning; they were well instructed in religious practices. So next morning they got up early and, after discussing it, they decided to start out to visit their father. When they saw the sun come up they said, "It's not far, just on the other side of the mountain." So they started that way, walking fast so as to get there quickly. They came to the top of the first range and saw another as far beyond as the first had been.

While they were talking about this someone spoke to them. It was kamashku koya (Spider Woman). She said to them, "My grandchildren, are you going to visit your father?" They were startled and said, "Did someone speak? Who is it? Who are you?" Spider Woman said, "Here I am." They looked in that direction and saw a spider on a bush. "Oh, is that you, Spider? Do you speak?" Spider Woman said, "Yes." So the boys told her they were going to visit their father. Spider Woman told them they were not to go yet, but to go tomorrow. Sun knew they were coming so he sent Spider Woman to meet them and instruct them how to reach him. So Spider Woman told the boys to follow her. When they came to her house, Spider Woman said, "This is my house, come on down." So they saw the spider go in and asked how they could ever go into such a small hole. Spider said, "Put your foot in, it will be large enough." So the older boy stepped in and the hole got large and they could see a stairway. He went on down and called to his brother, saying, "Come on, it is large enough." When they reached the bottom, there was a room and in it were many young spiders climbing around on the walls. They were afraid of the boys. Spider Woman fed the boys. She had just one boy in her family, so she asked this boy to collect webs from the other spiders, then to spin them into a ball so that it would reach to the house of Sun Man. Spider Boy brought back the ball. Spider Woman told the boys to rest for the night and to get to bed early for they were to start right after midnight, as they had far to go. So they went to bed early.

At midnight Spider Woman awoke Masewi and Oyoyewi and told Spider Boy to take the small basket (web) and to put the two boys in it and take them to their father's house, and to take good care of them and not to leave them till they arrived. So Spider Boy put them in the basket. The woman held one end of the ball of spun web and Spider Boy dropped down with the other, unwinding as they went. The boys were completely lost and did not know where they were, but they did not care much about that. Before the sun rose they reached the place where they were going. Spider Boy took them out of the basket and asked Masewi to let him crawl behind his ear where he could talk to him. Spider Boy gave them some roots to chew and rub on their bodies. This medicine was to protect them. "I will be along also to advise you," said Spider Boy. "You will spit toward the house where the Sun lives." Sun Youth knew his sons were coming, so he told his sisters who were with him that they were to arrive. He told them to wait for them.

The boys came to the base of the house and started to climb up the ladder. The women saw them and said, "Two boys are coming up. They look poor and dirty." One of the women said, "Maybe they are our brother's sons," but the others said," No, they can't be; our brother's children would be much better cared for." When the boys reached the top, they went right in (like Koshari) without ceremony. Sun Youth had a kiva, and one of the women went to tell him two boys had arrived, "Maybe they are your boys. Come up and see them." When the boys got in they asked for their father. By that time Sun Youth came in saying, "You have come, my sons." He picked them up and brought them down into the kiva. Sun Youth had brothers in the kiva and he spoke to them, saying, "My sons have come here." They laughed at the boys, saying, "Is that the kind of sons you have?" So one of the men asked if it was true that those boys were his sons. "If that is so, place them in the north den where the lions are and see if they come out alive."

So their father put them in with the lions. The boys were used to lions and were not afraid. Soon the lions began to lick them and act friendly. The boys played with the lions. One of the men got up to see if they had been eaten, and reported, "No, they are playing with the lions." So they were brought out. The man said, "Put them in the west den where the wolves are--they are always hungry." They did so and nothing happened to them; they came out alive. They were then placed in the south den with the lynx, [203] with the same result. Then they were placed in the east den with the bumblebees. The bees got all over them. One of the boys happened to open his mouth, one of the bees got in and he bit it, saying, "Oh, brother, they are good, they taste sweet." So they gathered others, breaking them open and sucking out the honey.

When the man came to see them he saw no harm had come to them and told them to come out. He reported the boys had killed a lot of their bees. They also had in the kiva a tsiwaimitiima [204] filled with hot coals. This is where the sun got its heat. Other kivas have their altars in this place. They were going to give the boys a final test. They grabbed the two boys and throw them into these coals, instead of being burned the boys came out full grown men, as handsome as their father. Now everyone was convinced that they were really children of the Sun. [205] They said they would send them back the next day, but in the meantime they would fix them up to be still more handsome. The boys had brought their bows and arrows. So the men took these and improved them. They put sinew backs on the bows and shaped them better. They put arrowheads and feathers on the arrows and made lion-skin quivers. They also made sticks (staffs) for them and told them they were going to be Country Chiefs. They put this staff in a special pocket in the quiver. They were told that with this staff they would be made strong and would be protected. (This is still a part of the quiver. It holds the quiver in shape.) This staff is called yapi [206] (pl. 16, fig. 1).

They were told they were to be strong rulers as representatives of the Sun. So their father also made for them a curved rabbit stick. He told them not to use it just anytime as it had so much power that they might destroy something. To use it only when it seemed necessary. If they killed something and felt sorry about it, they could place the stick (yapi) or an arrowhead (which was given them) on it and it would come to life. Their father also made for them eight arrows, four in each bunch, pointing out the ones they were to use only in an emergency. The other four could be used for hunting. He told them they were to be allowed everywhere, in the North, South, West, and East, even in the most sacred places, [207] and they would be listened to. "Whenever you want to come back to my house, the doors will be open to you." Then he said, "Now I will give you costumes which will make you handsome." So he gave them beaded moccasins, girdle, and sash (bokaı' yo). He gave them arm bands decorated with feathers. He gave them each a wrist band made of buffalo skin, that they were to wear always as a protection; they were never to take it off, as their heart would be in it. He gave them bead necklaces of turquoise and shell. "With all of these you will look handsome and will have power to attract." Then he painted them around the eyes with red paint, saying, "This is the way you will paint up for bravery."

All of this time Spider was coaching them, telling them not to be afraid in the different tests. Their father also made for them a headdress called heyeashuni to hang on the back of their hair. They were made a pouch to be carried by a strap [bandoleer] over the shoulder (pl. 16, fig. 2). In this pouch Sun placed a number of fetishes. [208] They were always to wear this. Finally Sun Youth looked them over and saw they appeared very handsome. "I have given you all that you need for bravery, good luck, and power," he said. He said they would stay overnight and go back the next day, when they were to accompany him with the sun. Spider Boy told them to agree. So they were taken from the kiva into the other room and given food. They passed the night there.

The next day Sun Youth took his sons and put them high in the sun. The sun began to rise and came over the horizon. Their father was talking to them and pointing things out to them as they looked down. They asked many questions, so that nothing would puzzle them. So their father said, "Now we are near your house." Sun Youth knew how they had come and knew that Spider Boy was still with them. So Spider Boy put them in a basket and their father held the other end of the web and it hung down. They told their father that they would do all that he had asked them and would follow his advice. As before, the boys were lost, not knowing how far they had come. They came right to the house of Spider Woman. The boys thanked Spider Woman and told her they had seen their father. So they said a prayer for her and left.

They returned to their house. Their grandmother and mother had been praying for them and feared they were lost and the lions had gotten them. They looked everywhere for them but could not find them. They were not recognized by their mother as they were now handsome grown men. Their grandmother did not believe they were the same boys, but they told how they had met their father and how he had given them names. After their grandmother and mother heard this they believed. The boys took off their costumes and hung them up, for they had been told not to wear them until they needed them. They made up ordinary costumes for themselves, and they continued to live as common people in the village.

PRESENT CUSTOMS OF ACOMA

SELECTION OF OFFICERS [209]

FOLLOWING the 4-day Christmas feast everyone gathers at Acoma, so on December 28 new officers are "elected." The Antelope Clan [210] has the authority to name the men. The Antelope clan selects about 2 months in advance. They select at least two men from each kiva so as to distribute the power evenly. They are careful to appoint so as not to be hard on any family. It puts a burden on the whole family when a man is appointed officer. They are careful to pick out a man who believes and follows the old traditions.

On the evening of the 26th, the officers who are going to resign call the chaianyi into Mauharo [the head kiva]; also two head men [211] of each kiva. The retiring Country Chief gets up and tells the chaianyi and representatives, "I have been given names of the men who are to take our places by Antelope clan nawai." [212] (The Antelope Man gives him this information and calls the meeting a day or two before.) He tells the council that he will name them and that this will be their chance to say whether they want each of these appointees. "If there are any objections, now is the time to present them." When the men are named, sometimes they all agree and sometimes some disagree and speak. The appointee most disagreed about is the one for Country Chief. This appointee must be physically strong, he must be conservative and not talk too much, he must be a good believer, and take the religion seriously. He should be a man who knows the tradition and its prayers. He must be a good runner, not lazy; he must be brave and a good leader. He must remain in Acoma and must remain rigidly continent. Each day he must visit all the kivas with his two lieutenants to see that all is in order. No one desires this Office. The other offices are more quickly decided upon.

The Country Chiefs: The first is called Tsatia hochani. The second is Shpati mut, "Mocking Bird. Youth"; being a brave man, he represents Masewi. He does the talking to the medicine men or to the heads of the kivas. He is the messenger, hence "mocking bird." The third chief is Shuti mut, "Wren Youth"; he represents Oyoyewi, the Younger of the War Twins. His duties are the same as those of Mocking Bird Youth.

Then there are two cooks (kupewi'tit, Sp. cocineros) who are under Country Chief. It is their duty to cook for the Country Chiefs, and to make corn meal for them. They represent the two helpers given to the first Country Chief by Iatiku. In the beginning there were only the [first] Country Chief and his two helper-cooks. But after Masewi and Oyoyewi left the Acoma people, two more Country Chiefs were appointed to take their place: Mocking Bird Youth and Wren Youth. The three Country Chiefs and their two cooks all live together. [213] They must observe continence.

From the meeting, Country Chief goes to Antelope Man and reports. If there has been any objection to an appointee, Country Chief explains why. In this event the council will name another man, but they must get Antelope Man to agree to the new selection. He can insist upon his candidate, if he wishes; usually he does not insist. Care is taken to make the appointment from a clan other than that of the retiring officer.

Country Chief says to the kiva heads, "Tell your children to wait till tomorrow. When you have eaten breakfast, come into the kiva and wait there."

If a man cannot be at the meeting, he must get consent to stay away, from the "father" or a chaianyi. Four chaianyi are appointed, two from the Fire altar and two from the Flint altar, to give out sticks of office to the appointees. The officers are always up early, they cry out and tell the women to get up early and cook breakfast, so the men can get to the meeting on time.

All the men are supposed to go, each to his own kiva. The four chaianyi go to Mauharo kiva. Then Country Chief goes to the different kivas and asks the head man of each if all members are present. When Country Chief has made his rounds, the chaianyi are first to leave the kiva. They go to the public meeting house. [214] They used to meet in the Mauharo (informant remembers it), but the chaianyi did not like any quarreling to take place in a sacred place, so they built the special meeting house.

Country Chief sends out his officers (the retiring officers) to get the different groups. The different groups are placed in different parts of the meeting house. Besides the retiring officers and the two officers of each kiva, no one knows who the new officers will be. After all are in, Country Chief asks the leaders if all of their members are present. They will report absentees and give the reason for absence. Country Chief acts as chairman and calls the meeting to order. He tells the people, "Now I am going to tell you that new Country Chiefs are to be appointed today and I will give them my staff." The officers still have their staffs with them, When they go to the meeting house, they take off their costumes[?] and, kneeling in front of the chaianyi, each hands him the staff with a prayer, "I give you back all your sacred clothes, all your rules, all your power, but I keep all the luck [215] that is in it [? the staff]. This will be mine." At this time they step out of office. Country Chief is free from responsibility, but he continues to preside.

First the five officers in the Country Chief's group are named. Next the tapu'pu (governor). He looks out for the people's outside affairs: public works, things not sacred or religious. Relations with other peoples are attended to by him. [216] He has authority to call meetings; in such matters he does not have to consult the Country Chief. In a matter such as furnishing men for the late [European] war, Country Chief would ask the governor to help him; but the reverse does not hold, as Country Chief cannot leave the pueblo.

The Governor has two assistants: Haukaupshi (one sitting next to him); and Chuitseesh (the last one). These two titles are preceded by tapupu: tapupu haukaupshi, tapupu chuitseesh. These assistants can take his place if he is sick. He consults with them, and they help out generally.

Next they appointed three pishka'ri (Spanish fiscales, no Indian name). Their duties are connected with the church. They have the key to the church, and sweep the church; they meet the priest and bring him in, help him, and call the people to church. When the pishkari wants work done on the church, he would be helped by the Governor. He also acts as helper and messenger to the Governor. The head pishkari has two assistants: Haukaupshi pishkari, Chuitseesh pishkari. These are all who are named at this time.

Country Chief will say, "If no one objects, you are to regard these men as your officers. They are the choice of the Antelope clan."

The people as a rule do not object. If one stood up saying, "I do not want this man," Country Chief would say, "All right, I appoint you!"

The people will say, "Thank you for the officers." The new men are given their staffs. The new Country Chief comes down and brings then, into the Middle. The chaianyi are all sitting on the south side. They say now which staff is to be given to each of the new officers. The man appointed to receive the staff kneels before the chaianyi, who holds up the staff and prays. This is a long prayer reciting how Iatiku gave power to these authorities. At a certain point in the prayer, the staff is handed over. The man meanwhile is praying also. He prays to Iatiku saying, "I am just a common man with no strength or authority. I have been appointed to this office and you will help me carry it out." The chaianyi blows on the staff four times, then passes it to the officer. The retiring Country Chief holds the hands of the new officer, raises him thus and seats him on the right side of the chaianyi. While the staff is being received the retiring officer rolls a cigarette which he gives to his successor. The retiring officers wait each for his successor and does likewise.

Frequently the newly appointed Country Chief will offer objections, but he is forced to take the position anyway. Frequently after 3 or 4 years one who was a capable Country Chief can be re-appointed.

After all the staffs are given out, the retiring Country Chief rises and makes a speech, telling the people that they must regard the now man as their officer. "I have finished my term." Sometimes he will relate what hard times he has had in calling out the people and advises them that they should have more respect for their officers and respond more promptly to their calls.

The new Country Chief then gets up and asks the people to regard him with respect as their new officer. All of the rest of the now officers get up in turn and make speeches to the same effect, naming the office they are taking over. Finally the new Governor gets up. He asks the people to appoint a man to be the "water boss." He usually names him ceremonially tsits tika kuwai'a nikouya (the one who orders the water). In common usage he is called mayordomo. There are four mayordomos. Formerly there were but two, but since ditches have been put in at McCarty's [217] they have needed four, one for each ditch.

After these men have been appointed, the new Country Chief prays, then gets up and adjourns the meeting. As the people pass out they say goodbye to [? shake hands with] the new officers.

The Governor has ten "principales" [218] as advisors. These men are named by the Antelope Man and hold office for life. They are distributed evenly among the kivas.

The next day the new Country Chief and his officers will meet and select a place for their headquarters. It may be the home of any one of the officers, usually a place with plenty of space and reasonable privacy. This is the way it is done now. Formerly it was always a house on the North side of the plaza (kakati). The relatives of the new officers replaster, whitewash, and shelve the room selected and, if it has no fireplace, they build one. After the room is finished and all is ready, the new officers go to the old Country Chief's quarters and receive from him the broken prayer stick and other paraphernalia which they transfer to their new room. The new officers then set a date and on it they go out and tell the people that the new officers want them to go out to get twigs for making prayer sticks; they tell them that their Country Chief is ready to work and that he wishes the people to help. The two cooks have to get any old corn left in the old country Chief's house and bring it to the new house. Their relatives build a corn grinding place for them. Their duty is to make sacred corn meal, and ka'nashaia, [219] a compound food ground up with matsit [matsinyi] or wafer bread and meat. Corn meal and kanashaia are to be used by Country Chief when he goes out to pray. The cooks have also to keep the place neat and well swept and always to have water in the room. They must do these things themselves as the room is regarded as sacred and even the members of the household are not allowed in it. One of these two cooks must always be in the room. Their duty also is to take the quivers in which Country Chief and officers carry their staffs, and put them on the officers' backs when they leave and take them off when they return. At night they spread the officers' pallets, which are made of only one pelt, so they will not sleep too soundly or in luxury. They must live in the old way, using earthen pots, logs for seats (passed on down, they have been worn down very low). Every time the officers go out they wear their bandoleer with bag of fawn skin into which the cooks have put the prayer meal and mixed food. It is the duty of the cooks to gather corn pollen in season, so as to have plenty for the office. They also collect pollen from cattails. This is put in pots and saved to last through winter. Corn pollen represents domestic plants; cattail pollen represents wild plants, and cattail is a water plant. This is all of the duty of the cooks.

Country Chief wishes help of people. Country Chief and his officers must dress in the old way, in buckskin clothes. They are not allowed to wear hats or any civilized clothes. When going out into the mountains to get branches for prayer sticks, they paint their faces like the Twins. When they get to the foot of the mountain, they say a prayer and scatter corn meal to make a trail into the mountain. Then they go on to the mountain singing a song, and when the bush or tree is found from which they are going to cut their prayer sticks, they again say a prayer to ask permission from the mountain, and ask the mountain not to blame them for doing harm. They tell the mountain that they came for the branches which will benefit the people. They ask yellow flint, blue flint, red flint, and white flint to cut the branches for them. Then they make a mark on the tree with a flint, after this they can cut it with whatever they wish. It is the rule for them to get as much as they can carry; it is to last them the whole year. The branches are tied with buckskin. All the way back to the village they sing their songs. At the foot of Acoma, they say a prayer and make a trail to take the branches into the village to be used for the benefit of the people, and then they go on into the village. The only ones who go after these branches are the two officers next to the head Country Chief. As soon as these two reach their house, the cooks help them down with their bundles. The head Country Chief makes the trail into the house with corn meal.

The next day the medicine man and two headmen of each kiva and the Antelope Man wait in their offices for the Country Chiefs to bring them the branches which they are to use for prayer sticks. When the Country Chief comes to the kiva he will call to be allowed to give the sticks to them, and he will name the place where he got them. The officers will say "yes" and take the bundle from the Country Chief who asks that these branches he used by them to help Country Chief.

The same day the Country Chiefs will sit in their house and make prayer sticks; the following day they will go out to pray for the first time. They will go out toward the north. These prayer sticks are all for different rulers, one for the North Mountain ruler [220] (pl. 17), four for the katsina at Wenimats (pl. 9, fig. 1), and three for the Clouds [these are the racing sticks (prayer sticks) and hoop and balls]. These different prayer sticks are placed in three different baskets along with corn meal, pollen, shells, turquoise, and cigarettes rolled with corn husks and wild tobacco. After dark, the three Country Chiefs paint themselves and as they paint they sing a song. The head chief and the one next to him paint up like the elder Twin and the third chief paints up like the younger Twin. This finished, the cooks help them with their corn meal container and quiver; they carry each a basket of prayer sticks on his back. At the doorway they stand and sing a song. After this they leave for the north to pray to North Mountain; they travel until midnight. [221]

They usually look for a spring. The first chief carries the prayer sticks belonging to the North Mountain ruler. The second chief carries the prayer sticks belonging to the katsina; the third chief, the ones belonging to the Clouds. When they get to the spring [222] each one unties his own bundle and prays to the one for whom the prayer sticks are intended. In these long prayers they name every blessing they can think of. A hole is dug in the spring and the prayer sticks are buried in the water and covered up with a stone slab. The first Country Chief brings along a canteen and gets water from the spring. They believe that when they get water from this real home of the water it will have magical power and be suitable for the medicine men to mix medicine. They also put a little of this water in every cistern on top of Acoma, so the water will last longer and so these places may attract the clouds or rain.

When they return to the village, before they get up on top, the two [assistant] chiefs separate and go back to their headquarters; the first Country Chief goes to the chief kiva, Mauharo kai. This night the chaianyi sleep in this kiva and they expect to be awakened by Country Chief. As soon as he gets to the opening in the roof, he asks to be allowed to enter. They say, "Come in!" He greets them saying, "Koatsi, mothers, and your officers, all is well, you are the leader." He has some turkey feathers tied up (wapani) [223] with which he prays to the north. He says a prayer. All the chaianyi listen and encourage him as he prays. As soon as he finishes his prayer he asks to be allowed to leave. They say, "All right, go from us in happiness and be brave." Going up and down the streets, he cries out to awaken the people. He goes to the east end where he starts praying to the Sun. Everyone gets up and with corn meal helps him to pray. He goes praying through the village. Then he returns to his house.

The cooks are waiting for him when he comes in. They greet him saying, "Have you come back, my son?" He breathes into the house four times, saying, "I have brought beads, harvest, game, long life, rain." The cooks are thankful and help him off with his quiver. They tell him to rest, saying, "You have done your work." He takes a short nap before sunrise. This is the first day. This day they rest. The next day they must again make prayer sticks. They make different sticks for the West. (It is not necessary to repeat the details of going to the spring.) On the return, the second Country Chief goes to Mauharo kai and then wakens the people. The next day they rest again and on the next day they repeat it all in connection with the South rulers. On their return the third Country Chief wakens the people. They rest again and the next day at night they go to the East, and the first Country Chief again wakens the people.

From this day they rest 8 days and then start taking turns, only one going out at a time now. They do not take the canteen, but only pray. Their prayers are for all the people. It is not only for the people of Acoma but for "everyone under the sun," haopate itini kaishpish (everybody on top where light is).

The duties of the people to the Country Chief: When called to do so they must bring wood; the women must make pikali--when the young women are asked they do this. The men must plant corn for Country Chief [224] and care for the crops. When there is no harvest, Country Chief can ask people to supply corn from their bins. From his supply he furnishes food to people who have no crops. The people also harvest Country Chief's crops. Country Chief may ask all the people to go out and hunt for him, when he is out of meat.

After the first Country Chief has completed his first prayer circuit, he reports to Antelope Man. Antelope Man says, "All right, son, I guess it's time for you to be initiated." [225] Antelope Man sets a date 4 days ahead. He tells Country Chief to make prayer sticks for Kapina chaianyi. All three Country Chiefs make these prayer sticks, leaving it to Kapina chaianyi to set up the altar. Kapina chaianyi says, "It is going to be for the good of my Country Chief and for the good of my people." There is just one Kapina chaianyi at Acoma so he usually asks the Flint chaianyi to help him. Kapina chaianyi sets the date 4 days ahead. During these 4 days he prepares his altar, setting it up.

On the morning of the fourth day usually all is ready. The Flint chaianyi do not bring their altar, but bring some of their paraphernalia, arrowheads, bear claws, etc. The sand painting used at this time is the one used when they cross the four mountains [226] (ashtiawakats). This painting is called "destroy tracks." Masewi and Oyoyewi went through this ceremony to get rid of their "haunt." The chaianyi go through this whenever they finish a curing ceremony. This means also that there is confession [? exorcism], wrong doings being forgotten on crossing the four mountains.

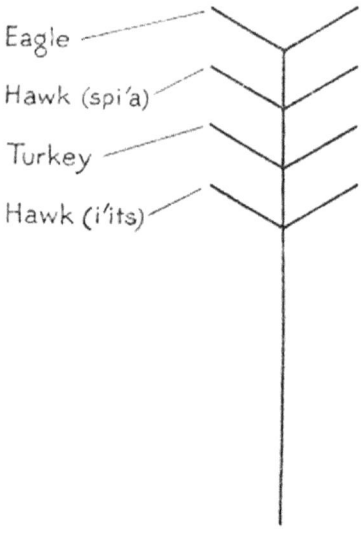

FIGURE 7.--Diagram of prayer stick of Country Chief.

Country Chief makes this prayer stick (fig. 7) representing eagle, turkey and two kinds of hawk: People who bring prayer sticks use only two feathers of any of the above birds. people understand that this altar is set up so you can obtain power to attract and kill game, to run well and be brave, and to be able to forget ills. These prayer sticks are to be taken to the altar to pray with. To attend any chaianyi work, it is necessary to dress in the old way in breech cloth and blanket, carrying prayer stick in hand. Hair is cut in the four-cornered way (fig. 8) because Iatiku so instructed, as four corners represent any four time period necessary to fulfil or complete. The parting which separates bang from long hair represents the Milky Way, because the Milky Way holds you up. Hats cannot be worn in kiva as the Milky Way must be exposed and not hidden. Shoes are not worn in kiva. One may not pray in shoes; shoe tracks represent "mule tracks." That is what the katsina say.

FIGURE 8.--Ritual hair cut.

When all is ready, Country Chief goes into the street and cries out that all is ready and the people may go to the kiva. It is not compulsory. Nowadays not many people attend. Forty years ago it drew a full house. [227] The people do not go right in but wait on the roof until time to enter. Country Chief goes in first and has his prayer stick put into the fetishes; the three Country Chiefs do this. Hunters take their bow or gun to get power. As soon as one enters, he goes up to the altar and goes to the tiamuni [228] tsamaiya, either the male or female. The chaianyi stand on each side of them, singing. When you finish the prayer, you give the feathers from the prayer stick to the chaianyi who forces them into the tsamai. [229] When you finish your prayer, you step back and sit. The chaianyi leads you all over the sand painting by his feathers. This goes on until everyone has crossed the four mountains. Some of the chaianyi are singing all the time.

Now comes the time to be clothed with whatever blessing you wish. The sand painting is swept up with feathers, then the yucca frame and the Yucca leaves that were spit in two, are taken out at once and carried to the south end of the mesa, where they are thrown into a large crevice.

At this time one Kapina and one Flint chaianyi go into Mauharo kai where they dress up like katsina, but without masks. When the song has been sung and it is time, one of the chaianyi goes after them. They come out of the kiva giving the katsina yell and the war cry of the Twins. They rush into the kiva where the people are. One of the Kapina chaianyi holds the basket and the Kapina chaianyi do a fast shuffling dance over the tsiwaimitiima, making a lot of noise. When they finish this foot shuffling, the Kapina stand one on each end and one holding the basket in the center. The first Country Chief is asked to step out. Then all four start to dance, keeping time with the song. After the first song, they shuffle their feet again. Then the Kapina woman holds up the basket, giving it to the Country Chief, and steps back. Then the Kapina standing on his right strikes him with a yucca switch four times in front on shins, thighs, stomach, chest; the Kapina on the other side strikes him similarly four times from the back.

Everyone else present then goes through the same rite. This completes the most important part. Another song and the people are given back their bows and hunting sticks, which had been placed on one side of the altar by the medicine men when they came in. Then they go home. While going out each person is given a drink of the medicine mixed by the chaianyi. All leave except the three Country Chiefs. The chaianyi ask them if they are manly enough to drink the tsi'chuni medicine they have prepared. It is made out of the dung of snakes. If the Country Chief drinks this, it will give him the power to foresee things. He is asked if he will drink this. Some do and some do not. [230] Four days after drinking it he must stay in kiva. The chaianyi rather hope none will drink it, as they too must stay in these 4 days. No one may touch or help the one drinking the medicine, not even touch his blanket. Anyone touching him will fall and be badly injured. He does not fast during this time. He can speak to anyone and leave the kiva for necessities. During these 4 days the chaianyi give Country Chief advice and relate the traditions. They instruct him in relays, first one chaianyi, then another. This finishes the Country Chief's initiation.

KATSINA INITIATION [231]

THIS initiation goes back in place to White House where the real katsina left and the katsina society was organized. Acoma people do it exactly the same today.

This ceremony usually follows a little after the dramatization of the katsina fight; now it is early in April. Every 5 years the dramatization is held, and after every second dramatization (every 10 years) the, initiation is held. It is called the initiation of the children (i'achniamanwatsi'watruma, "young initiated to be").

Country Chief asks Antelope Man if it is not time to initiate the children. (Girls and boys both are in this. This is initiation into the tribe.) [232] Antelope Man says, "Yes, it is time." They keep watch for the sunrise from the east end of the mesa. There are different points on the east mesa, where the sun comes up. The sun is watched from a certain rock; the horizon is on the east mesa and marked with small gaps. When the sun reaches a certain place, Country Chief knows it is time for the initiation. So he sets the date and tells the people, especially all who have a child about 10 years old (more or less from about 6 years to any age).

The father and mother watch out for this. It is the parents' duty to select someone to be a "father" to the child, to present him for initiation. The father makes up a prayer stick with which to approach the man he is going to ask to act as "father" to the child. Two days before the ceremony, the father goes to the house of the man he selects. Usually he selects a friend and he speaks to him as "brother." He asks him if he will act as "father" to the child, naming him with clan name. [233] He brings also corn meal and ground up mixed food and cigarettes. The man says a prayer accepting the child. It is customary to bring a large amount of corn meal, as the person accepting must take some of it to all his relatives because this child is to become a son of all of his clan, and each of his relatives (everyone, men, women and children) takes some of this corn meal and goes out and prays for the child. Country Chief appoints a man to represent Tsitsanits, the katsina chief, from hai'mata'ata [234] kiva. Country Chief also selects two Gomaiowish from the same kiva. (A man belongs in the kiva of his father.)

They are to dress up with masks representing their parts. At this time (the morning of the second day before initiation) the Antelope clan's altar is set up in Mauharo kiva. Country Chief helps bring in the altar. Country Chief then leaves, and guards the kiva. The Antelope clan nawai gets some of his clan members who know the songs and in the afternoon they are brought into Mauharo kiva. Later the two Gomaiowish come in, talking busily. They have come from the west. Antelope clan nawai waits for them in his office [235] and they go there, reporting to him that they have come, because, "You have called us. Tsitsanits is on the way and will be here later. We are coming to initiate the children. We came ahead to bring the medicine (plants, roots, branches, etc.)."

The Gomaiowish then leave, going up and down the streets talking, They look at the ground, saying, "There are lots of tracks, there must be lots of children here!" They say, "Some of them have no moccasins, but after they are initiated, we will bring them moccasins." The children are usually frightened half to death. (The talking is for the benefit of the children and to quiet their fears.) After they have done this, Gomaiowish enter Mauharo kai. There they dance to the singing of the Antelope clan, smoking, talking while they sing, making the people laugh. Just before sundown, they ask permission to go back for Tsitsanits, who is late. They joke, saying they are going to weigh the children and measure them. "But I guess they are not coming till Tsitsanits arrives, so we had better go get him." So they leave.

That evening, at sundown, the man who is to be "father" to the child goes to one of his relatives to get him to help by putting the feathers on the heads of the children when they come out from the initiation. The Gomaiowish leave their medicine in the kiva and the "father" goes and gets a little piece of each kind. This medicine is to keep the children from being afraid. Later in the evening all the people enter their kivas. When the time comes, the Country Chief comes around to the kivas telling the "fathers" to get their children and bring them to the chief kiva.

The "fathers" and their helpers take the children to the kivas. Other men go out to meet Tsitsanits. They go to the west end of the village and wait there. A short distance southwest of Acoma is where Tsitsanits and Gomaiowish dress. You can hear their cries as they approach. Before this the men who are not "fathers" ask their women to boil some corn for them, as they are going to act "katsina" to present corn to the children in kiva. They hand it down, but do not enter the kiva. They are not masked, but the children do not see them. They hand down apples, corn, etc., which the "fathers" reach up and get.

As soon as Tsitsanits comes past these men, they pray, saying, "He is the only one who is real; we are only guards." They all make a lot of noise like katsina, so it can be heard in the kiva. The man acting as father, when he comes to the home of the child, chews some of the medicine, spits it over the child and says, "I have come for you, my child." He gives some to the child, telling him, "Eat this and you won't be afraid." The parents encourage the child. The child is carried from its threshold on the back of the "father" all the way into the kiva. They are placed where they won't get lost. One man can be "father" to two or three children; in this case they have to hurry so as to get them in before the katsina arrive. The katsina are not dressed and they believe that if they see the katsina not masked it will give them the itch and body sores.

Antelope clansmen are singing all this time in the kiva. When the children hear the noise outside, they get frightened. When Tsitsanits arrives on the roof, he yells and scratches, while the Gomaiowish make all the noise they can. A buffalo skin closes the entry. This skin is painted with katsina masks on the inside of the skin.

Antelope Man stands under the ladder. He has a ball of ashes mixed with food (corn meal and pollen). When the song ends he throws this ball up against the skin. The Gomaiowish then open up the skin and Tsitsanits dashes in as fast as he can, followed by Gomaiowish. This is acted out to seem as if the ball knocked off the skin cover. The Gomaiowish make a lot of racket. Tsitsanits shuffles his feet over the tsiwaimitiima. Antelope Man dips his feathers into the medicine and sprinkles Tsitsanits and the Gomaiowish. This quiets them down a bit. Antelope Man then says, "Tsitsanits has come to initiate our children." Tsitsanits makes gestures of agreement. The ones sitting near on the right side of the ladder go up first to the altar. There is a rush to get there first. The "father" leads the child by the hand to the front. Tsitsanits stands on the west side, the, "father" on the north side, and the child stands on the tsiwaimitiima. Tsitsanits strikes the child four times (across shoulder, back, thighs, legs). Then they turn around, the "father" stands on the tsiwaimitiima (still holding the child) and it is his turn to be struck. Then the one who is to put on the feather, a turkey feather, steps up and puts the feather in the hair of the child. If a man has more than one child, he puts them through one after the other. (Iatiku also told them to cut children's hair, all but a topknot to which the feather is tied. Their hair is cut thus until this initiation. After this it can grow long. That is why children want to go through this early.) The man tying on the feather first pulls up eight times on the topknot--so the child will go over four mountains (meaning long life). The feather is to be worn 4 days. Turkey feathers are used on prayer sticks as a guard and this hair feather is a guard for these 4 days. On the fourth day the child takes it off with a prayer. During these 4 days the "father" gets the measurement of the child's feet and makes moccasins for him (or her) and buckskin clothes (a whole new outfit).

On the fourth day the katsina will come. The Gomaiowish tell the children, before they leave, that in 4 days the katsina will come bringing them presents. It is customary for the Mixed katsina to come. Any number can come from each kiva. Their masks are brought to Mauharo kai. In kiva the "father" is making moccasins. The "mother," the wife of the "father," is making up the clothing. Early in the morning of the fourth day, the "mother" goes to the house of the child and brings the child to her house. They have there in the house, set in baskets, the outfit for the child: if a boy--bow and arrow, hunter stick, and clothes; if a girl--clothes and the rainbow head ornament (uaishtiakayani) [236] (pl. 13, fig. 1). [237] When the children are brought in, the "mother" uncovers the basket, saying, "This has been sent you by the katsina. The crows brought it from Wenimats." (Children seeing crows, look at them to see if they are carrying presents, The "stockings" of the katsina represent crow stockings. Parents point out the crows to the children, saying, "See, the katsina are going to come!" [238] Katsina presents are left outside the door, to get children up early, and parents will say, "See what your brother found! Let's see to whom it belongs." The children try on the different things to see for whom each thing is intended.) After the presents are made, the "mother" washes the head of the child and gives him a feast (on the floor).

Meanwhile, just before the katsina are to come, the chaianyi have been placing their altars [? in the kivas]. They bring the children in front of the altar and give them a bath to give them new life. This finishes the initiation.

A general feast will follow. The "mothers" prepare the corn meal which is brought to the "fathers" by the real fathers as payment for service. The initiate will regard his "father" as a real father; and all the relatives of the "father" will be considered relatives.

KOSHARI INITIATION [239]

MY informant's father was chief of Koshari, and he told members that when he died he wanted his oldest son to take his place.

When the time came, the Koshari told his mother that they wanted him. His mother told him there was no way out of it, since his father had wished him to take his place. So he consented, and his mother told the Koshari head man. When the Koshari had a meeting, they came after him. He was taken to the haima kaach (the kiva used by the Koshari as a meeting place). So the head Koshari told the young man and the four other initiates to come and make prayer sticks, as it was time for the Country Chief to have his doings. It was time for the ceremony when the warriors renew the scalps. It was customary to initiate the Koshari at this ceremony. (Nowadays they catch them temporarily for any ceremony. [240] My informant's initiation was the last one.)

The, old Koshari had sticks they were going to make prayer sticks of, pins for women's skirts (pl. 13, fig. 1). Each Koshari was to make four extra--four for the women to dance with and four to pray with, so they had to make a great many. They also made cigarettes of corn husks with each set of pins. The old men were present while they were making these.

They stayed in the kiva 4 days. On the fourth day, in the morning, they set up the altar with two honani, many stuffed wrens (shuti), and mocking birds with one grain of corn inside for the heart. There were different kinds of herbs and medicines, also some flints and a stone fetich in human form with cotton all around the face. This represented the mother of the Koshari.

The ceremony started with a song. At a certain place in the song, they all chewed herbs and spat into a pot which contained the white clay they were to use as paint. They had to sing four songs during this. Then one got up and mixed the paint--clay, herbs, saliva, etc. The initiates stripped and started to sing again, and at another point in the song, the old men painted them and fixed them up like Koshari. It took quite a while to paint them.

After it was finished the old men fixed and painted themselves.

They had a square medicine bowl. They started a song to make medicine and they started to mix medicine. Everyone was chewing herbs and spitting in the bowl at the proper times.

When it came time, one of the old members took a dish, urinated in it and mixed this with the medicine; another put phlegm from his nose in it, and the woman who was a Koshari pulled out some pubic hair and threw it in. After all this was mixed the head man took some in his mouth and spat it over all the other Koshari, then the initiates did the same, then everyone took a drink of the medicine from a shell. (After drinking the medicine, four drinks each from the shell, they were full fledged koshari.) Then the initiates stood in a row at the foot of the ladder. The head man said, "Follow me, we are going to call the people in the kiva tonight." Then the head man prayed and made the trail of corn meal out to the ladder. He asked the power of the real Koshari to be with all of them so they would not be injured in any way and would have the wit of the real Koshari.

Two initiates paired off in one direction; two, in another. The leader led them up. He started quick, three steps at a time. When h' got on the roof, he gave a yell and jumped up making a noise. Then they went down the outside ladder. At the bottom they lined up and started to sing. (Some are dirty songs, some are really comical.) They made a round of all the streets singing. Then they came into the plaza dancing (i. e., acting as if they were dancing). When the song and dance was finished they gave, a yell and scattered out, going from house to house telling the people to meet in the Mauharo Kai.

The ceremony took all day. It was about sundown when they finished the round of the houses. Then they returned to the kiva and got about half undressed. The leader told them to go back to their houses and get haati (sweet meal) in a bowl and bring it back and pass it to the leader, who would mix it in a large bowl with water. He would mix some of the medicine with each batch. A lot had to be made as many people were to be present.

It is customary for people to gather a little after sundown. The leader asks if they are all in. Koshari are in full costume. The medicine food is mixed in another room (not the kiva) with a stick made of cactus used as a torch so, as the medicine is passed around, they can see in the dark. Then another Koshari lights a long cigarette made of reed stuffed with tobacco and with honey on the end. This is handed to the first one in the row. This is a special Koshari cigarette. When you have taken a puff, it means you are bound to the Koshari and must do as they wish. Two bowls of food are passed around, and a lot of cigarettes. Each member smokes one. During the ceremonial period one cannot make a cigarette of his own.

Following this, the ceremony of the scalp dance is held.

During the 8 days before the ceremony is over, the initiates are instructed what to do. Before going out, all the stuffed wrens from the altar are put in bags and a bag is hung around the neck of each Koshari, the badge of Koshari. The wren is worn only during the ceremony. These wren and mocking bird skins mean you will have the power of chattering and talking like these birds.

BIBLIOGRAPHY

BAILEY, VERNON

1931. Mammals of New Mexico. U. S. Dept. Agric., Bur. Biol. Surv., North American Fauna, No. 53.

BANDELIER, A. F.

1890. Final report. Pap. Archaeol. Inst. Amer., Amer. Ser., vol. 3.

1918. The delight makers. New York.

1940. Pioneers in American anthropology: The Bandelier-Morgan Letters, 1873-1883. Ed. by Leslie A. White. Coronado Cuarto Centennial Publ., 1540-1940. Albuquerque.

BEALS, RALPH L. See PARSONS, ELSIE CLEWS, and BEALS, RALPH L.

BENEDICT, RUTH

1931. Tales of the Cochiti Indians. Bur. Amer. Ethnol. Bull. 98.

1935. Zuñi mythology. Columbia Univ. Contr. Anthrop., vol. 21.

BOAS, FRANZ

1928. Keresan texts. Publ. Amer. Ethnol. Soc., vol. 8, pts. 1 and 2.

BOURKE, J. G.

1884. The Snake Dance of the Moquis of Arizona. New York.

BUNZEL, RUTH L.

1932. Introduction to Zuñi ceremonialism. 47th Ann. Rep. Bur. Amer. Ethnol., 1929-1930, pp. 467-544.

CULIN, STEWART

1907. Games of the North American Indians. 24th Ann. Rep. Bur. Amer. Ethnol., 1902-1903, pp. 3-846.

DENSMORE, FRANCES

1938. Music of Santo Domingo Pueblo, New Mexico. Southwest Mus. Pap., No. 12. Los Angeles.

DUMAREST, NOËL

1919. Notes on Cochiti, New Mexico. Mem. Amer. Anthrop. Assoc., vol. 6, No. 3.

FEWKES, . WALTER

1902. Minor Hopi festivals. Amer. Anthrop., n. s., vol. 4, pp. 482-511.

FORDE, C. DARYLL

1930. A creation myth from Acoma. Folk-Lore, vol. 41, pp. 359-387.

GATSCHET, A. S.

1891. A mythic tale of the Isleta Indians, New Mexico. Proc. Amer. Phil. Soc., vol. 29.

GOGGIN, JOHN M.

1940. A ball game at Santo Domingo. Amer. Anthrop., n. s., vol. 42, pp. 364-366.

GOLDFRANK, E. S.

1923. Notes on two Pueblo feasts. Amer. Anthrop., n. s., vol. 25, pp. 188-196.

1927. The social and ceremonial organization of Cochiti. Mem. Amer. Anthrop. Assoc., No. 33.

GUNN, JOHN M.

1917. Schat-Chen; history, traditions and narratives of the Queres Indians of Laguna and Acoma. Albuquerque.

HODGE, FREDERICK WEBB

1896. Pueblo Indian clans. Amer. Anthrop., n. s., vol. 9, pp. 345-352.

1907. Acoma. Article in Handbook of American Indians. Bur. Amer. Ethnol. Bull. 30, pt. 1.

KROEBER, A. L.

1917. Zuñi kin and clan. Anthrop. Pap. Amer. Mus. Nat, Mist., Vol. 18, pt. 2.

LOWIE, R. H.

1938. The Emergence Hole and foot drum. Amer. Anthrop., n. s., Vol. 40, p. 174.

MINDELEFF, VICTOR

1891. A study of Pueblo architecture: Tusayan and Cibola. 8th Ann. Rep. Bur. Ethnol., 1886-1, 887, pp. 3-228.

OETRO, NINA

1936. Old Spain in our Southwest. New York.

PARSONS, ELSIE CLEWS

1917. The Antelope Clan in Keresan custom and myth. Man, Vol. 17, No, 12, pp. 190-193.

1918. Notes on Acoma and Laguna. Amer. Anthrop., n. s., Vol. 20, pp. 162-186.

1918 a. War God shrines of Laguna and Zuñi. Amer. Anthrop., n. s., Vol. 20, pp. 381-405.

1919. Census of the Shi'wanakwe Society of Zuñi. Amer. Anthrop., n. 8., Vol. 21, pp. 329-335.

1920. Notes on ceremonialism at Laguna. Anthrop. Pap. Amer. Mus. Nat. Hist., Vol. 19, pt. 4.

1920 a. Notes on Isleta, Santa Ana, and Acoma. Amer. Anthrop., n. s., Vol. 22, pp. 56-69.

1923. Laguna genealogies. Anthrop. Pap. Amer. Mus. Nat. Hist., vol. 19, pt. 5.

1923 a. Notes on San Felipe and Santo Domingo. Amer. Anthrop., n. s., vol. 25, pp. 485-494.

1923 b. The origin myth of Zuñi. Journ. Amer. Folk-Lore, Vol. 36, pp. 135 162.

1923 c. Fiesta at Sant' Ana, New Mexico. Scientific Monthly, Vol. 16, pp. 178-183.

1924. The scalp ceremonial of Zuñi. Mem. Amer. Anthrop. Assoc., No. 31.

1929. The social organization of the Tewa of New Mexico. Mem. Amer. Anthrop. Assoc., No. 36.

1936. Early relations between Hopi and Keres. Amer. Anthrop., n. s., Vol. 38, pp. 554-560.

1939. Pueblo Indian religion. 2 vols. Univ. Chicago Press.

1940. Taos tales. Amer. Folk-Lore Soc. Mem., Vol. 34.

PARSONS, ELSIE CLEWS, and BEALS, RALPH L.

1934. The sacred clowns of the Pueblo and Mayo-Yaqui Indians. Amer. Anthrop., n. s., Vol. 36, pp. 491-514.

ROBERTS, FRANK H. H., JR.

1932. The village of the Great Kivas of the Zuñi Reservation, New Mexico. Bur. Amer. Ethnol. Bull. 111.

SETON, E. T.

1929. Lives of game animals. 4 vols.

STEPHEN, ALEXANDER M.

1936. Hopi journal. Columbia Univ. Contr. Anthrop., vol. 23.

STEVENSON, MATILDA COXE

1894. The Sia. 11th Ann. Rep. Bur. Ethnol., 1889-1890, pp. 3-157.

WASHPA

1910. Article in Handbook of American Indians. Bur. Amer. Ethnol. Bull. 30, pt. 2.

WHITE, LESLIE A.

1930. A comparative study of Keresan Medicine Societies. Proc. 23rd Int. Congr. Amer., 1928, pp. 604-619.

1932. The Acoma Indians. 47th Ann. Rep. Bur. Amer. Ethnol., 1929-1930, pp. 17-192.

1932 a. The Pueblo of San Felipe. Mem. Amer. Anthrop. Assoc., No. 38.

1935. The Pueblo of Santo Domingo, New Mexico. Mem. Amer. Anthrop. Assoc., No. 43.

1942. New material from Acoma. Bur. Amer. Ethnol. Bull. 136, Anthrop. Pap. 33. 1

MS. The Pueblo of Sia.

MS. The Pueblo of Santa Ana.

WINSHIP, GEORGE PARKER

1896. The Coronado Expedition, 1540-1542. [Narrative of Casteñada.] 14th Ann. Rep. Bur. Amer. Ethnol., 1892-93, pp. 329-613.

PLATES

EXPLANATION OF PLATES

(These plates have been reproduced from water color paintings by an Acoma Indian. The colors of the originals are described in the explanations.)

PLATE 1

Acoma katsinas

PLATE 1, Upper Left

UPPER LEFT: Morityema, ruler of West Mountain. Eagle-feather prayer stick and topknot of parrot feathers; circle represents a blossom with colors of the four directions; snout of wood with rabbit fur; collar of crow feathers. Greenish blue (turquoise) color of West Mountain and of Spring.

PLATE 1, Upper Right

UPPER RIGHT: Maiyochina, ruler of South Mountain. Red is the color of South Mountain; green represents summer crops. (Impersonator looks through the mouth, not the eyes.) Rabbit fur around snout; parrot-feather topknot-, turkey-feather rosette with fan of eagle feathers; owl-feather collar; blue yarn over forehead.

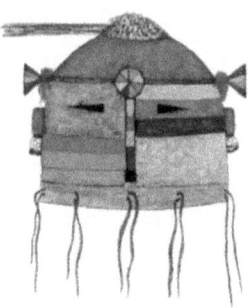

PLATE 1, Center Left

CENTER LEFT: Oshach Paiyatiuma, Sun Youth. Parrot feathers; three squash blossoms; median line is the trail over which Sun goes; blue for sky; striped quarters for the rainbow around Sun; eagle-feather earrings; buckskin thongs are to fasten a spruce-twig collar.

PLATE 1, Center Right

CENTER RIGHT: Kuashtoch katsina. Green, the color of mountains; terra cotta forehead and back; two eagle feathers, one parrot feather; squash blossom of gourd or yarn; blue yarn on forehead with abalone shell pendant; spruce collar.

PLATE 1, Lower Left

LOWER LEFT: Tsitsanits, Katsina chief. Green for sky; yellow for earth; black for night; topknot of breast feathers of parrot (every katsina has this); at back, eagle feathers spread out like an eagle's tail; horns of wood to represent buffalo horns; red yarn; eyes are balls of stuffed buckskin painted white; slits under the eyes for the impersonator to look through; teeth of corn husks; beard of human hair; fox-fur collar.

PLATE 1, Lower Right

LOWER RIGHT: Shuracha, Corn clan katsina. Black because he is a fire maker and is smoked up; spots are the direction colors; turquoise earrings; cotton sash (paniu) around neck; designs suggest katsina heads. (Since the katsina are secret, they do not picture them entirely. Here only the shape of the head is indicated; in pls. 11, figs. 2, a, and 6; fig. 2 only the eyes.)

PLATE 2

Plate 2

Acoma, viewed from the roof of the Convento.

PLATE 3

Plate 3, Figure 1

FIGURE 1. Antelope clan altar. Oak crooks (brown) with eagle feathers (white with black tips); turkey feathers (white with black tips) on end of hook; masks, left to right--(1st) Shuma'ashkă (face green, rest brown); (2nd) Ahote (black, ears blue); (3d) Gomaiowish (brown on green base); (4th) Kuashtoch (face blue, features and cap black, base green); (5th) Gaupakta (brown with green cap); medicine bowl (outside brown with black edge, inside white with brown lines); stone points (gray).

Plate 3, Figure 2

FIGURE 2. Shakak, ruler of North Mountain. Crest of eagle feathers (white with black tips); blue for sky (right side of mask); yellow for earth (left side of mask); collar (light brown) and rosette (black and white) of owl feathers. Mouth outlined in green.

PLATE 4

Plate 4, Figure 1

FIGURE 1. Shruisthia, ruler of East Mountain. Eagle-feather prayer stick (black and white); parrot-feather topknot (red and green); blue yarn over forehead ending on either side in brown earrings, with tassels of turkey feathers, blue tipped; mask, black (for night); and white (for the East); lower edge brown.

Plate 4, Figure 2

FIGURE 2. Tsiukiri, father of the Kopishtaiya. Turkey feathers (gray with white and black tips) as earrings and back of mask; parrot-feather topknot (green and red); slanting line (red) represents the direction of the southeast that Tsiukiri followed when sent away by Iatiku; the short line joining it (red) is the straight East-West direction; the spots (green, red, blue, orange, and white) are direction colors; the background is black because the Kopishtaiya are night spirits; turkey tracks (white) in the snow make it easier to track the turkeys, so are lucky; fox-fur collar (gray); eyes and mouth outlined in red.

PLATE 5

Plate 5, Figure 1

FIGURE 1. Kuapichani katsina. Wearing full katsina costume; eagle feathers (white with black tips), stick (black) with humming bird (red); parrot-feather topknot (red and green); ears (brown) painted as usual the color of the forehead (brown); spruce collar (green); turquoise earrings; abalone-shell pendant; coral necklaces (red); black torso and white lower body represent night and day; arm bands of buckskin with spruce (green); green buckskin belt; kashpa (black and white), ceremonial sash with tassels; hotsini (white with black border), cotton kilt; in right hand gourd rattle (quartered in orange, red, green, blue); in left hand flute (striped red and white with zigzag design in green, black, and white) with gourd (center, orange with cross; edge, white with green design) on the end; garters (blue) with turtle-shell rattle (brown); moccasins of buckskin (white with red toes).

Plate 5, Figure 2

FIGURE 2. Hachamoni kaiok (broken prayer stick). The face (yellow, hair black with white feather on top) represents Iatiku; the feathers are eagle down, and under them is cotton; body brown; first necklace, shells; second, coral; third, coral beads with three abalone-shell pendants.

Plate 5, Figure 3

FIGURE 3. Koshari. Hair (black) tied with corn husks (yellow); earrings (black) of lizards; necklaces of dried apples (brown) and of rabbit skin (white and black); shoulder straps, bracelets, and anklets of spruce (green); girdle of buffalo-hoof rattles (black); turtle-shell rattles (white with black markings) on knees (ordinarily they are worn behind the leg but Koshari wears them wrong in front); feet painted (in black) to represent moccasins.

PLATE 6

Plate 6, Figure 1

FIGURE 1. Nawish katsina. Eagle feathers (white with black tips); parrot-feather topknot (green and red); forehead brown edged with blue yarn; face painted with colors of the directions: orange (background of face), the earth, yellow (stripe at upper right), the Sun; green (center stripe at right), water; blue (lower stripe at right), the sky. The terraced design (white edged with red) represents a field; red yam around mouth; lower edge of mask with thongs for fastening, brown. A spruce collar will be worn.

Plate 6, Figure 2

FIGURE 2. Kopishtaiya. No special name; referred to merely as "the one who carries clouds on his head." Hennati, cumulus clouds (white with triangular black marks and edged with red with dependent black lines); black horizontal line is wakaianish, the black line under the clouds when it is about to rain; the black vertical lines are rain; lightnings (red); blue (right side of mask) for sky; yellow (left side) for earth; turkey tracks (white); diagonal line and short line joining it (red); lower edge of mask red with brown thongs for fastening. Turkey feathers (black and white) in ears; eagle-down feathers on the Clouds (shi'wana)

PLATE 7

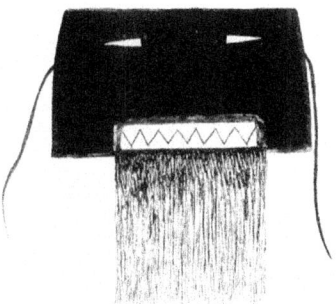

FIGURE 1. Chakoya katsina. Mask black bordered with brown; eye-slits yellow; blue feathers from duck head around the mouth; teeth of corn husks; beard of human hair. A skirt of an entire buckskin hanging almost to the feet will be worn.

Plate 7, Figure 2

FIGURE 2. Shumaashka, Corn clan katsina. Squash blossom (red) on side; horn frame (green) strung with cotton; blue (left side of mask) for sky; yellow (right side) for earth; median line represents a 4-day trail with black and white for night and day; sash collar (white) with pendant ornaments (blue and red).

PLATE 8

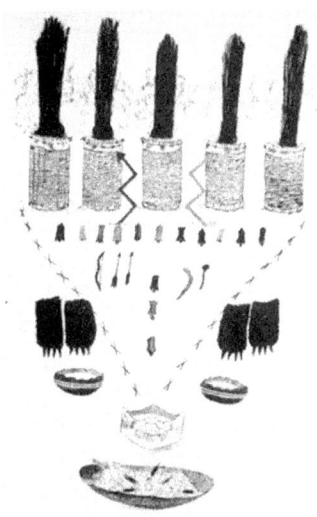

Plate 8, Figure 1

FIGURE 1. Hunters' society altar. Five honani [241]; two lightnings (right, yellow; left, red) (the power for killing game: yellow, north lightning; red, south lightning); fetiches of carnivorous animals; down the center is the hiamuni (corn meal road) which the animals follow to go out; two pairs of mapani (left bear paws, black); bows, arrows, rabbit sticks (brown); bowls of sacred corn meal (orange with white bands); medicine bowl (white with tan design); basket (brown) of prayer sticks (white feathers, variously colored sticks). The tracks (black) of the road-runner are made so the rabbits won't know which way the hunter is heading.

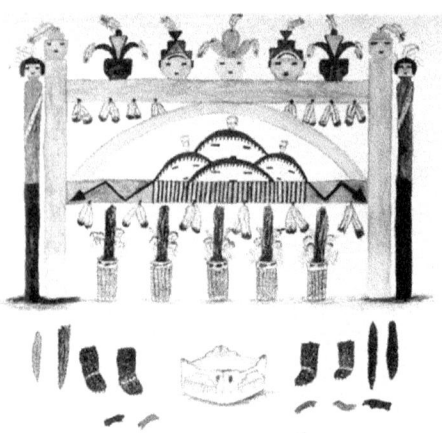

Plate 8, Figure 2

FIGURE 2. Fire society altar. The frame (green), ichini, is the house of everything on the altar; on right end, Masewi (face yellow; hair black; three feathers white; body brown and black; diagonal twisted rope white); on left end, Oyoyewi (face blue, otherwise coloring same as Masewi); the arc (buff) is the Milky Way; over it the middle figure is Iatiku (yellow face, 3-lobed tan headdress, feathers white); on each side Kuishanako, Blue women (blue faces; forehead white with curved black stripe; headdresses, green triangle in stepped black design topped with white feather); the next two are Kuganinako, Red women (red faces; headdress, orange triangle surmounted by green ball; black petals on either side suggest fleur-de-lis; feathers, white); the two end ones (tall) are Kochininako, Yellow women (faces tan, body and headdress green, feather white). (These women are the mothers of the first-born girls, clan mothers, the first to be born after Iatiku.) The feathers (white, black-tipped) from the horizontal bar represent rain; under the Clouds (white, rims red fringed with black, feathers white) the lines and the suspended feathers (white, black-tipped) also represent rain; at each end, lightning (red); the five corn fetishes at the bottom are honani (Iatiku) [242] ; in front, the medicine bowl (white with tan design; inside white with yellow border); on each side, left paws of bears (black) and stone points (gray, brown) used for killing; in front, stone fetishes (black, gray, brown) of Bear, Lion, Wolf. etc.

PLATE 9

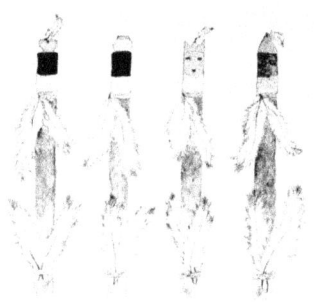

Plate 9, Figure 1

FIGURE 1. Katsina prayer sticks. Made of willow (a "water" tree); the bark is left on and the lower part (brown) represents legs; measured from base of palm to tip of middle finger (about 7 inches); turkey feathers (white), on top eagle down; the faces are painted in the colors of the directions (from left to right--1st, dark green; 2nd, red; 3d, yellow; 4th, light green); section below faces painted blue for sky and represents the body; top pieces: two (1st, yellow; 2nd, white with tan decoration) represent a jar; two (tan), a mountain.

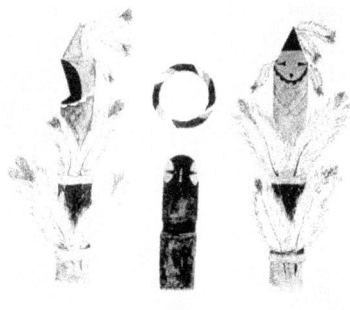

Plate 9, Figure 2

FIGURE 2. Fire society prayer sticks. Upper center: Basket ring (maskuch) to put on the head for Iatiku to use; it is painted with the colors (diagonal bands of red, white, yellow, blue) of the Mountains of the four directions. Lower center: The prayer stick (blue, with green and yellow top) represents Iatiku, with belt (green) and pot rest, the two things she asked for; the befeathered sticks (brown; sections between feathers, green; scalloped design at base, white) the chaianyi decided of themselves to offer; the cones (left, green and brown; right, black and yellow) on top represent mountains; the turkey feathers (white) are the clothes (whenever things are tied to a stick, they are clothes).

PLATE 10

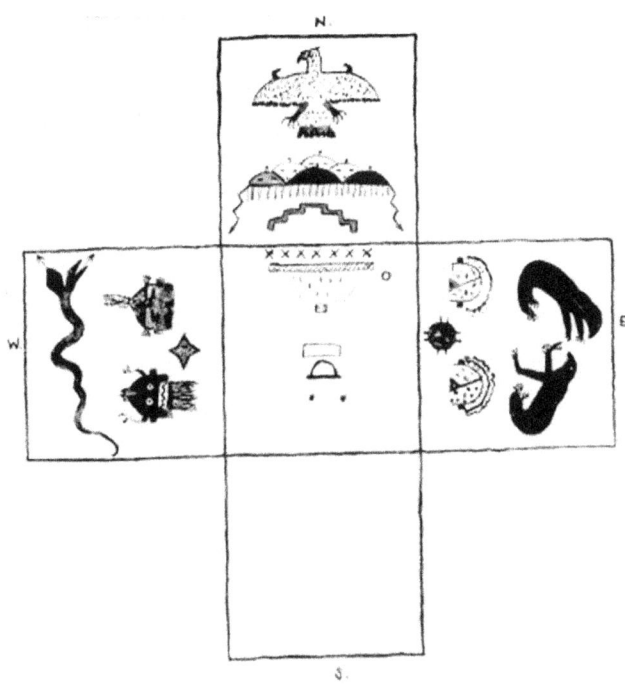

Plate 10, Figure 1

FIGURE 1. Kiva floor and murals. Central panel shows floor with medicine men (X X X) sitting behind altar, with shipapu kuwatsaishuma (O), medicine bowl (▫),, tsiwaimitiima(▫), fireplace (⌒), ladders(H H).North wall: Flint bird (white with black and brown dots, legs and tail brown), Clouds (upper three, white; lower three, orange, blue, red) and lightning (red) over field (orange). West wall: Water snake (brown) (killed by the Twins), Tsitsanits katsina (half blue, half black; forehead black divided by red triangle, horns green), Oshach katsina (blue face, green forehead, feather top piece); star (brown). South wall always left blank. East wall: Bears (left, black; right, brown) (note hearts, also two shamanistic eagle feathers in left paw); Kopishtaiya, Sun (red, with black "rays"); Kopishtaiya katsina (see pl. 5, fig. 2); Tsiukiri katsina (see pl. 3, fig. 2). People sit in an are around south, southeast, and southwest walls.

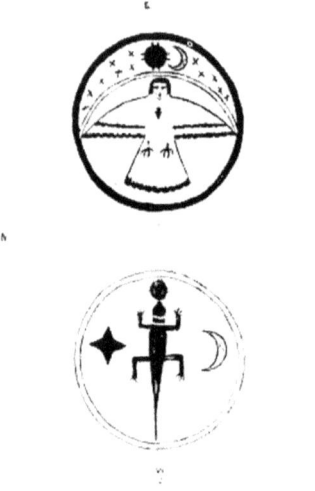

FIGURE 2. Altar sand paintings. a, Fire society altar: The rim (blue) is the sky; the upper crescent contains the symbols for the sun (red), moon (yellow), and stars; the arc (pale gray) is the Milky Way; the face (yellow with black hair) below, Iatiku; and the spots (yellow) represent the earth; the triangular object (red) on breast is the heart, the center of the earth and the center of the picture. b, Ant society altar: Circle (pale gray) and spots (yellow) are of corn meal; star, blue; sun, red; moon, yellow. The lizard (green with 4 bands--yellow, blue, red, white--around throat) can eat ants and gives power to cure a person afflicted with itching caused by ants.

PLATE 11

SUN and Moon paintings (These figures are used in sand painting or on kiva wall to get power from Sun and Moon.)

Plate 11, Figure 1

FIGURE 1. The Sun. The face is red because the Sun is male and the giver of strong light; ornament on forehead (brown and black triangles, divided by white line) represents a squash blossom; two outer rims are green and orange; projections (orange) represent beams of light.

Plate 11, Figure 2

FIGURE 2. The Moon. The face is yellow because the Moon is female, and the light is pale; the two outer rims (green and red) are the "ring about the moon"; ornament (brown and black triangles, divided by white line) represents a squash blossom.

PLATE 12

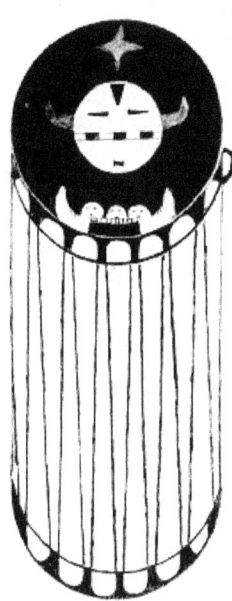

Plate 12, Figure 1

FIGURE 1. Drum. Sides are yellow with vertical blue lines; band at base, blue with white scallops; top blue; katsina symbol in center of top, yellow with green and white band and hornlike projections of red; boatlike object lower edge of top, yellow with blue in middle section; star on top, yellow. Symbolism of colors: Blue for sky, yellow for earth. Boatlike object represents clouds resting on horns. Corn or seed are inside drum to be the heart.

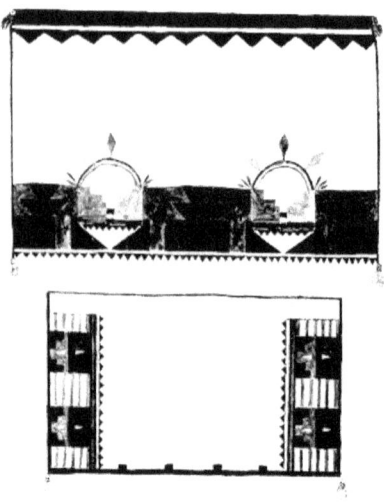

Plate 12, Figure 2

FIGURE 2. Katsina costume. a, Mantle of impersonator of female katsina, Made of cotton; the design is embroidered on one side with colored yarns; top, black and green in 4-day period; white line is a trail; serrations top and bottom represent waves of water; white body represents the earth. Unfinished (no eyes) katsina masks; the diamond (red, yellow) represents feathers on the mask, the terraces (red, yellow) on the mask face represent fields; the median line on the face represents the 4-day-and-night period. b, Kilt worn by impersonator of male katsina: Designs are fields (red, blue) with part of katsina face. Straight lines (red) for rain, water; bottom line (black) for the 4-night period.

PLATE 13

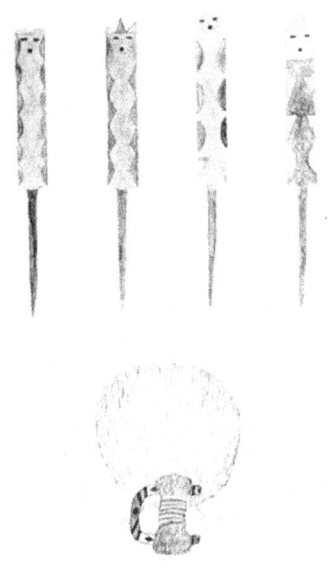

Plate 13, Figure 1

FIGURE 1. Maiden's hair frame (design in green, red, blue, yellow, white), Koshari prayer sticks; from left to right: 1st, face and body pink, scallops blue, top piece yellow, stick brown; 2nd, face and body yellow, scallops green, top piece blue and green; 3d, face yellow, body pink, scallopspurple, stick brown; 4th, face white, top piece yellow, front design green, sides blue and yellow, stick brown.

Plate 13, Figure 2

FIGURE 2. Objects on Kapina society altar. Tsamaiya (Tiamuni). Yucca blades (hatuni) for whipping (green). Bowl (white outside, brown inside) for sacred corn meal with design of the four Mountains of the color directions (yellow, blue, red).

PLATE 14

Plate 14, Figure 1

FIGURE 1. Prayer sticks used by Kopishtaiya, also Antelope clan staff. a, Trail (hiamuni) prayer stick (gray and blue). It opens the trail; it is laid so that the head faces the pueblo. The Kopishtaiya use it in entering the pueblo. b, Shield (haiitsi) of Kopishtaiya, a hoop (brown) with cotton string (black) fastened like a star. c, Staff (yapi) (pink) the Antelope clan use in the drama of the katsina war, willow (see p. 87). d, Used as a cane (gray) by Tsiukiri, Kopishtaiya chief. Turkey feathers at tip of crook (white), eagle and parrot feathers. e, This hiatsimuh prayer stick (brown, feathers red) laid by the Kopishtaiya against corners of houses and cliffs to keep them from falling. Hard wood. Four of these are used at a time. The paint iakatcha (manly paint) they get from Hopi. Faces above a and c green.

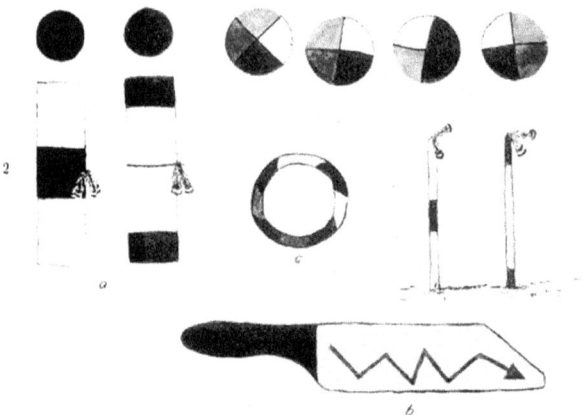

FIGURE 2. Miniature ritual implements. a, Kick sticks (black and white) with prayer feathers: about 4 inches; face (green) of the katsina summer cloud ruler on ends. b, Tokia moti. Colors on the balls (quartered in red, blue, yellow, white) are for the four directions; the paddle is black (handle) for night, yellow (blade) for earth, red for lightning (on blade); miniature goal stakes (white and black). c, Miniature pot rest (blue, yellow, red alternating with black) for Iatiku.

PLATE 15

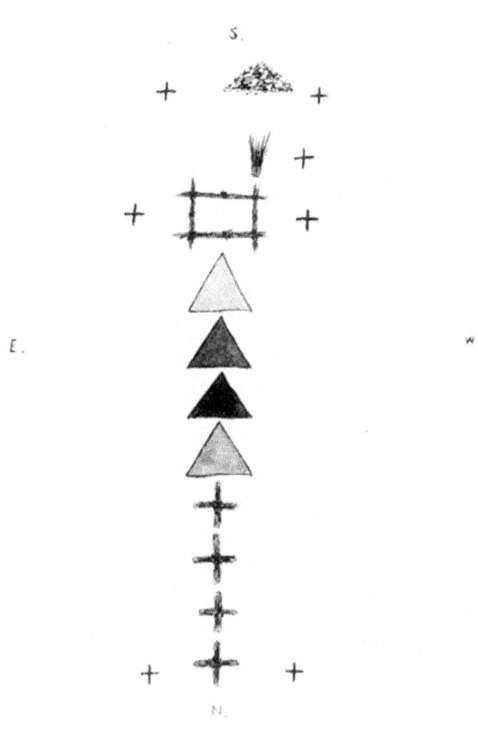

Plate 15, Figure 1

FIGURE 1. Sand painting and paraphernalia for exorcism (gray, red, blue, and yellow triangles; green crosses, frame, and grasses).

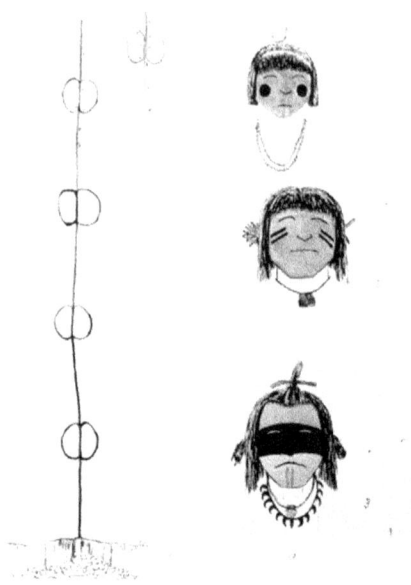

Plate 15, Figure 2

FIGURE 2. a, Face paintings of the dead. 1, Woman (face yellow, red spots on either cheek, necklace coral). 2. Man (face brown). 3, Chaianyi (forehead tan, mask black, lower part of face grey; clan necklace black and abalone pendant gray). b, Groove in rock for rite of forgetting the dead.

PLATE 16

Plate 16, Figure 1

FIGURE 1. Weapons (waiishi) given by Sun to the Twins. a, Dart used before any other weapon; corn cob (brown), large and burned and smoothed with stone; wood foreshaft (black) with arrowpoint (gray); feathers of any kind. b, Throwing stick (chaipichama), hard wood (brown) with lightning design (gray). c, Club of hard wood (brown), chaitsi (rabbit-club root). d, Otiawani of hard wood (brown). e, Arrow of achïti wood (brown); eagle feathers (black) and arrowhead (gray) tied with sinew. f, Bow of oak (brown) with sinew back; string of sinew which is laid out flat, wet, then twisted up.

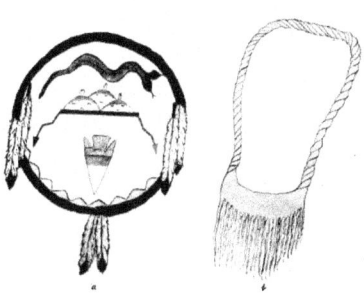

Plate 16, Figure 2

FIGURE 2. Shield and pouch of the Twins. a, Shield of buffalo hide; the two-headed water snake (brown) that the Twins killed at the time of the flood; stone point (tip white, butt yellow, with 2 lines, blue and red above) that Lightning (red) tried to kill them with, the colors representing the different kinds of stone points that were used; bottom, water waves (blue); eagle feathers. b, Pouch (light tan).

PLATE 17

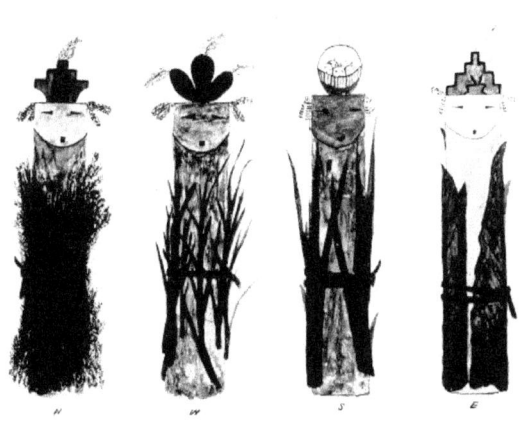

Plate 17

Prayer sticks for the Mountains of the four directions.

N: Spruce wood (brown; face yellow) and twigs; headdress (center black, outlined in green, sides red, top edged with green), symbol of snow for winter. W: Pine (brown; face blue); o'kai reeds (green) from early spring water plant; headdress (center lobe black, side lobes green), symbol of early leaves for spring. S: Fir(?) (brown, face red); cattail leaves (green); headdress, symbol of jar, clouds (face, white) and water (green) for summer. E: Aspen (gray, face white); corn leaves (green) ("the clothes"); headdress, symbol of field (red terrace outlined in black; lightning symbol in black) for fall. Turkey feathers at ears of all four prayer sticks; eagle down at top.

ENDNOTES

[1] All Keresan pueblo origin myths that have been collected so far begin in the same general way and follow essentially the same pattern: In the beginning the people were in the interior of the earth; there were two women, sisters; the people emerge from an opening in the north, migrate southward, etc. (p. 4)

[2] Boas, (1928, pt. 1, pp. 221, 222, 228; pt. 2, pp. 10, 11) reports a spirit at Laguna known as Ts'ιts'tc'i·'na·'k'o, "Thought-Woman." Gunn (1917, 1, 89) speaks of Sitchtchenako, who is "creator of all." At Sia we find Sûs'sĭstinnako, who is also a creator. and is said to be a spider (Stevenson, 1394, pp. 2c~-27). A spirit named Tsi'tyosti·nako is reported from Santa Ana (White, ms.). (p. 4)

[3] Diacritical marks will be noted only in the first use of a term or in terms quoted from published sources. (p. 4)

[4] From kut'tsiti, crammed full (in the basket); the implication being "nothing lacking". (p. 4)

[5] At Santa Ana the cicada is called tsi·k'ă. In the Santa Ana origin myth the badger and the cicada assist in preparing for the emergence as they do here (White, ms.). (p. 5)

[6] This is the only instance of translations of these names thus far reported. In many Keresan origin myths Ï'tc'ts'it$^{y'}$i and Nau'ts'it$^{y'}$i are sisters. At Laguna, according to Boas (1928, pt. 1, p. 221) Ï'tc'ts'it$^{y'}$i has been transformed into a man, "the father of the Whites." He attributes this change to Catholic influence. (p. 6)

[7] This may be another instance of adaptation of a Catholic idea to Indian form. latik, the great mother, deity of the Keres, lives in the interior of the earth, "four worlds down." (p. 6)

[8] The narrator belonged to the Sun clan. (p. 7)

[9] Mouse (Mus musculus) and rat (Rattus norwegicus) are called si'ya'na at Santa Ana (White, ins); the latter is so called at Santo Domingo (White, 1935, p. 203). (p. 11)

[10] See k'a·'TSα, kangaroo rat (Dipodomys spectabilis), in Boas (1928, pt. 2, p. 92, II. 2, 5, 7)--L. A. W. (p. 11)

[11] Nī·ty', prairie dog (Cynomys ludodvicanus), Santa Ana (White, ins.); Santo Domingo (White, 1934 p. 203); Laguna (Boas, 1928, pt. 2, p. 247, l. 5). (p. 11)

[12] For mountains at the cardinal points: k'awe·'cT^{y}ιmα, tspι'Dα, Tau'T^{y}umα and k'tc'α'nα (Boas, 1928, pt. 1, p. 283). (p. 11)

[13] ya·'won^{y}i, Laguna (Boss, 1928, pt. 2, p. 2, l. 1). (p. 11)

[14] T^{y}aits^e Pinus edulis, Laguna (Boas, 1928, pt. 2, p. 244, l. 7); gyai'ts^i, Santa Ana (White, ms.). (p. 12)

[15] Identified as western redtail hawk (Buteo borealis calurus, Cassin) at Acoma (White, 1942), as Swainson and Ferruginous roughleg at Santo Domingo (White, 1935, p. 204), and as sharpshinned hawk (Accipiter velox, Wilson) at Santa Ana (White, ms.). (p. 13)

[16] Identified at Acoma as western goshawk (Astur atricapillus striatualtus). (p. 13)

[17] Identified at Acoma as sharpshinned hawk (White, 1942). (p. 13)

[18] Cro·'k'aiya, Santo Domingo (White, 1935, p. 205); cro'wakaiya, Santa Ana (White, ms.).
(p. 15)

[19] tyε'nyε' (Boas, 1928, pt. 2, p. 286). (p. 18)

[20] k'wa'ya (Boas, 1928. pt. 2, p. 292). (p. 18)

[21] Archaic term for white now used at Acoma only ceremonially, chămŭts being the word commonly used. At Santa Ana, kăshăish is commonly used.--L. A. W. (p. 18)

[22] It has been called Mustard or Tansy Mustard. (p. 18)

[23] Ca·'k'ak' who lives on North Mountain (Boas, 1928, pt. 1, p. 283) and sends snow (p. 19).

[24] At Laguna Mo·'rit^{y}αmī lives on the mountain of the nadir (Boas, 1928, pt. 1, p. 282). (p. 19)

[25] Laguna, cui'siyai (Boas, 1928, pt. 1, p. 283); Santo Domingo, crui'simana'wi (White, 193.5, p. 32). (p. 19)

[26] These names for the seasons correspond with the Santa Ana terms, except for Fall; the Santa Ana term is sto·na (White, ms.). (p. 19)

[27] Informant's note: The rulers of the Mountains look fierce, different from the katsina. Shakak looks like a boss. Shruisthia is not a very good fellow. He brings soot and rubs it on the faces of people. (p. 19)

[28] "Big teeth," or "The whipper." He whips the children when they are initiated into the kachina cult. This kachina is reported from Laguna but not from any other Keresan pueblo. (See White, 1932, pp. 72-74, 79, pl. 10, b; 1942; Boas, 1928, pt. 1, p. 279; Parsons, 1920, p. 100, fig. 10; Gunn, 1917, pp. 127-123.) (p. 19)

[29] Reported from Acoma and Laguna but from no other Keresan pueblo. A full company appears In dances. (See White, 1932, p. 75, pl. 4, d; Boas, 1928, pt. 1, p. 279; Parsons, 1920, p. 100.) (p. 19)

[30] A full company of KoaBi'tacnyi appears in dances (see White, 1932, p. 75, pl. 4, b.) Unreported from any other Keresan pueblo. (p. 19)

[31] A full company of Wai'oca appears in dances at Acoma (White, 1932, p. 75, pl. 4, f.). Duck katsina are found in most, if not all Keresan pueblos. (p. 19)

[32] Jemez katsina (see White, 1932, p. 75, pl. 5, d.). (p. 19)

[33] Informant's note: Before going to work in their fields, Acoma people call upon Nawish to help them. Nawish guard the fields. At Wenimats Nawish are themselves farmers.
A full company of Na·'wic appears at Acoma (White 1932, p. 76, pl. 2, e.). This katsina is found in most Keresan pueblos. (p. 19)

[34] This is the first time Bear katsina has been reported from Acoma. He is found at Santo Domingo (While, 1935, pp. 107, 111) and at Cochiti (Goldfrank, 1923, p. 112). (p. 19)

[35] He appears at Acoma today in the "Fight with the katsina." He lives on the south side of the Acoma mesa (White, 1932, pp. 79-80, pl. 2, f). Unreported from other Keresan pueblos. (p. 19)

[36] Gomaiowish are to be equated with the Koyemshi of Zuñi (Parsons, 1918, pp. 182-183; 1920, pp. 101, 103). (See White, 1932, pp. 79, 89-91, 130, 144, 148, pl. 10, b; 1942; Parsons, 1920, fig. 15; Boas, 1928, pt. 1; p. 278.) They have been reported from Sia and Santa Ana (White, mss.). but not from Santo Domingo, San Felipe, Cochiti. (p. 19)

[37] Moki or Hopi katsina. A full company appears at Acoma (White, 1932, p. 75, pl. 10, f). Reported at Laguna (Boas, 1928, pt. 1, p. 279), but not from other Keresan pueblos. (p. 19)

[38] They are the best moccasin makers; men call for them when making moccasins (Informant's note). (p. 19)

[39] At Acoma this term (K'o·Bictai'ya) refers to (1) a health and strength-giving supernatural and to (2) masked impersonations of these supernaturals who appear at Acoma in the winter time. In no other Keresan pueblo are these spirits impersonated so far as is known. In Keresan pueblos other than Acoma K'o·Bictai'ya seems to be a generic term for benevolent spirits. (See White 1932, pp. 79, 86-88, pls. 8, b, 10, a; 1942.) (p. 20)

[40] In Keresan mythology We·nimats[i] is the home of the katsina and it is located "out in the west." (See White 1932, pp. 69, 142; Boas, 1928, pt. 1, p. 277; White, 1932 a, p. 24; 1935, pp. 173, 175; Dumarest, 1919, pp. 172-173. (p. 20)

[41] See White 1932, pp. 125-129. (p. 20)

[42] Cf. koai'k'tc', Boas (1928, pt. 1, pp. 284-285). (p. 21)

[43] Meaning of nano unknown. ūs'thĕ suggests the Acoma pronunciation of Dios, yo·cthi (White, 1932, p. 128). ai'tcin means "house" at Santo Domingo (White, 1935, p. 9), also the wooden slat altar. Compare pl. 16. (p. 21)

[44] See White, 1942. (p. 21)

[45] The cacique at Acorns today is the head of the Antelope clan and the "father of the katsina" (White, 932, p. 41). (p. 21)

[46] At Acoma and Laguna the wooden slat altars of the curing societies are called yaBaicini (White, 1932, p. 109, ftn. 1) or ya·'paicī'n[yi] (Boas, 1928, pt. 2, p. 61, l. 16). Among eastern Keres the meal-and-pigment paintings are so called; the wooden slat altars, ai'tcin (White, 1942; 1935; ms., pp. 11, 161). (p. 21)

[47] See White, 1941 a, for the ritual of delivering and receiving a message from the Gomaiowish. (p. 22)

[48] They are met today in all Keresan pueblos (except Laguna) by the cacique (see White, 1935, p. 95; Dumarest, 1919, p. 177). (p. 22)

[49] The head kiva. (Cf. White, 1932, pp. 30-31; Boas, 1925, pt. 1, p. 293.) Among eastern Keres the k'a·'atc' is called tci·'kya (White, 1935, p. 11; 1932 a, p. 15). (p. 22)

[50] Informant is explaining that mauharo is the ceremonial word for kiva, k'a·'atc' the ordinary word; kai means house. (p. 23)

[51] The opening into the upper world through which the people passed when they "came out" is usually referred to as Shipapu (cip'áp^u Laguna, Boas. I", pt. 2, p. 1, l. 1). But, strictly speaking, Shipapu is the place in the fourth world below, inside the earth, where the people were at "the beginning." The actual place of emergence is called Gauwatsaicoma (White, 1942). See also pl. 10. fig. 1. (p. 23)

[52] See White (1932, pp. 31, 49, 73 and fig. 2, p. 73) for the, tsiwai'mιtyιn, "foot drum," and its uses. Something quite like this is reported for Zuñi (Parsons, 1924, p. 21), among Hopi (Stephen, 1916, pp. 10, 17, 514, 704), and at the Village of the Great Kivas near Nutria (Roberts, 1932, pp. 58-60. cf. Lowie). (p. 24)

[53] See White, 1932, pp. 101-102; 1942; Boas, 1928, pt. 1, pp. 28-33, 296-298. (p. 25)

[54] Compare the Santa Ana tale about a man who got power from a witch to kill a deer. The hunter put the shell given him by the witch in the deer's tracks and performed a ritual. When he caught the door "its legs were scorched up to his knees and when they ate the meat it tasted like it had been smoked. The Caiyaik' found out about the way this man had killed his deer, and made him quit it. They took his shell away from him and destroyed it. They say the Navahos and Comanches used to kill deer like this." Compare First Mesa hunt fire (Stephen, 1936, pp. 1006, 1024, fig. 501). (p. 26)

[55] Communal hunts for small game are almost always to provide food for the katsina and for fetishes, See Boas, 1928 pt. 1; pp. 296-97; White, 1935, pp. 144-46. (p. 28)

[56] The vulva or the penis and testicles are placed in the stomach (White, 1942). (p. 28)

[57] The word co·ho·'nα (Boas, 1928, pt. 2, p. 42, l. 2), eastern Keres: ro'hona, is difficult to identify; it has been rendered lynx, weasel, jaguar. I am strongly inclined to believe that this animal is the jaguar. In a Santa Aria myth ro'hona is distinguished front mountain lion and front wildcat, and he is large enough to kill an antelope. One Santa Ana informant identified ro'hona as a jaguar from a colored picture in a manual on mammals of North America. In Boas' Laguna myth, "The

origin of hunting customs," co·'ho·na is distinguished from mountain lion and from wildcat and is large enough to knock down a mountain sheep. Therefore this animal must be fairly large and powerful.

Moreover, the co·'ho·na is assigned to the south, the direction of the home of the jaguar, with reference to the Pueblos.

The jaguar was formerly found occasionally as far north as the Pueblo Indian country although his customary haunts are farther south. On April 10, it is reported that a jaguar killed four men in a convent at Peña Blanca (Seton, 1929, vol. 1, pt. 1, pp. 28-29 (p. 31)

[58]Cf. Laguna (Parsons, 1920, p. 127, fig. 20).
(p. 31)
[59] This corresponds closely with a recent account from Santa Ana (White, ms). Deer skulls and horns, with feathers attached to the antlers, could be seen in great numbers on the roofs of houses at Sia a few years ago. (p. 32)

[60]Usually translated "outside chief, country chief." (p. 33)

[61]Nowadays the war chiefs are selected without reference to clan affiliation in all Keresan pueblos.
(p. 33)
[62] Cf. White, 1932, p. 46; Boas, 1928, pt. 1, p. 288. (p. 34)

[63]Informant's note: It is the center pole, four earths down and four sides up, which holds the skies and the earths in place so they will not give way or slip aside. Skies and earths are meant to last forever and this keeps them in place. Every year when prayer sticks are made, the broken prayer stick is renewed, and asked to start the new year fresh again and strong. For 4 days Kapina chaianyi renew it, and repaint it. The beads are taken off and buried and new beads put on by the new war chief. (p. 34)

[64]This is a common figure of speech for officers among the Keresan pueblos. It is, of course, equivalent to our "under your wing." (p. 34)

[65]Cf. White, 1932, p. 50. (p. 34)

[66]Canyon wren (Catherpes mexicanus conspersus, Ridgway). (p. 34)

[67]Western mocking bird (Mimus polyglottos leucopterus, Vigors) (White, 1942). (p. 34)

[68] Cf. White, 1932, p. 41. (p. 35)

[69] Cf. White, 1932, pp. 84-88. (p. 35)

[70] Cf. White, 1932, p. 86 and pl. 8, b. (p. 35)

[71] This term looks very much like taBinock^a, "homed toad" (White, 1932, p. 150) and mĭt^y, "youth." (p. 36)

[72] At Santa Ana obsidian is pulverized and soaked in water to bathe sore eyes (White, ms.). (p. 37)

[73] Medicine men are able to effect cures only because they are able to secure power from the "real" medicine men, the animals: bear, who is the greatest of doctors, badger, eagle, wolf. See White, 1930, p. 609; Steven. son, 1894, p. 72, telling how the original animal doctors initiated the first human medicine men (White, 1935, p. 121). (p. 38)

[74] mai'Dyup^i is identified (White, 1942) as black-footed ferret (Mustela nigripes) or as shrew (Sorex) (Stevenson, 1894, pp. 73. 128). A Santo Domingo Indian identified mounted specimens of Sorex personatus and Blarina brevicauda, as mai'Dyup^i (White, 1935, p. 203). (p. 38)

[75] All medicine men who treat sickness caused by witches in Keresan pueblos wear bear-skin paws on their hands-sometimes on both hands, sometimes on the left only--in treating patients or in fighting witches. See White (1942) for an account of how a medicine man skinned a bear. Medicine men also wear necklaces of bear claws. (p. 38)

[76] These are the hi'cami with which medicine men extract witch-injected objects from sick people, exorcise evil spirits, or sprinkle medicine water. (p. 38)

[77] See White, 1932, pl. 1, b; and fig. 5, p. 130, for pictures of Acoma medicine altars. (p. 38)

[78] She is referring to the so-called shell mixture that, with corn meal or pollen, is sprinkled on the ground. (p. 39)

[79] Cf. Densmore, 1938, pp. 40-45. (p. 39)

[80] The cotton-wrapped, bead- and feather-decked corn ear fetish of the Keresan curing society. See Acoma (White, 1932, p. 129); Sia (Stevenson, 1894, p. 4k,, ftn. 1, l. 9); Laguna (Parsons, 1920, pp. 95-96); Santo Domingo (White, 1935, p. 161);

Cochiti (Dumarest, 1919, p. 155). It represents the mother of the Indians, Iatiku, and is also called yaya, "mother." Among eastern Keres it is called ia'riko. Honani is the Hopi word for badger, although the accent is different: Acoma, ho'nani; Hopi, hona'ni. (p. 39)

[81] Called koto'na in other Keresan pueblos. Cf. the Hopi term chochĭmĭnga (Stephen, 1936, Glossary). (p. 39)

[82] In Sia mythology Iatiku, before taking leave of her people, instructed Tiamoni to make an iariko "which was to represent herself that they might have herself always with them and know her always" (Stevenson. 1894, pp. 40-41). (p. 40)

[83] Many Santa Ana prayers ask for rain, long life, etc., "as far as my prayers can reach" (White, ms.). (p. 40)

[84] Sp., guaco, waco, Rocky Mountain Bee plant, Cleome serrulata (or Peritoma serrulatum). It is tabu to the Shikame-Kurena medicine society at Laguna (Parsons, 1920, p. 112, ftn. 3); to the Shikame society at Cochiti (Dumarest, 1919, p. 189) and at Santa Ana (White, ms.); also to the Shi'wanakwe of Zuñi (Parsons 1919, p. 333).(See Robbins, Harrington, and Freire-Marreco, 1916, pp. 58-59, for Tewa uses.) (p. 40)

[85] Cf. White, 1932, p. 47.
(p. 42)
[86] Paraphrases? (p. 42)

[87] Cf. White, 1932, pp. 114-115. (p. 43)

[88] Colors, spirits, and mountains are associated with the cardinal points. In almost all rituals one begins with the north, then passes to west, south, and east. Songs are sung for each direction, this is to get power "from the whole world" and to concentrate it at the point where the medicine man wants to use it. (p. 43)

[89] Witches "shoot" thorns, rags, or broken glass into people's bodies, causing illness. (p. 44)

[90] Medicine men use a quartz crystal called ma·'caiyoyo to obtain second sight. (See White, 1942.) (p. 44)

[91] See White, 1932, pp. 111, 120, for disposal of "disease objects." (p. 44)

[92] Informant's note: During the ceremony, when one doctor tires of curing he sits down while another takes his place. When he sits down be is given a cigarette by

the official cigarette roller (who is selected when the 4-day fast begins). When the doctor takes the cigarette, he says, "kaumu" (join, this word is used only during ceremonies, for everyday use the word shattsi is used). The cigarette roller repeats the same word. When the doctor accepts the cigarette, the roller says, "Shanaish-tyu, my father." (p. 44)

[93] I know of no case in which a Koshari as a koshari assists medicine men in a curing ceremony. (p. 44)

[94] Cp. White, 1932, pp. 116-120. (p. 44)

[95] Sutanaiyic means our mother. (p. 44)

[96] In Sia mythology, the Kapina society is referred to as Spider society; it was composed of Spider people. Sûs'sïstinnako, a spider, was its first head (Stevenson, 1891[4], pp. 26, 39-40, 69).
The Acoma Kapina society was a very important society. Among other things they initiated the war chiefs. They had war functions (White, 1932, pp. 42, 48-49, 107, 117 ftn. 15; 1942). (See also Boas, 1928, pt. 1, pp. 64-67, 139, 291.) Parsons (1936, pp. 556) sees close relationship between the Acoma-Sia Kapina societies and the Hopi Snake-Antelope societies. (p. 44)

[97] Recruiting members for the secret societies is a common practice among the Pueblos. For Acoma, see White (1922, pp. 111-112, and 1942); Santo Domingo (White, 1935, pp. 131-132); San Felipe (White, 1932 a, p. 18); Cochiti (Goldfrank, 1927, pp. 52-53); Tewa (Parsons, 1929, pp. 128-129); Zuñi (Kroeber, 1919, p. 167). (p. 45)

[98] Cf. White, 1932, p. 97; 1935, pp. 30, 52; 1942. (p. 45)

[99] Cf. White, 1932 a, p. 17, and Stevenson, 1894, pl. 10, A; White, 1935, pl. 3. (p. 45)

[100] Cf. White, 1932, p. 48; 1942. The fetishes are called Tsamai'ya and Tsamahi'ya. In general, these terms refer to (1) spirit warriors (Stevenson, 1894, p. 130), to (2) war chiefs in Keresan pueblos (Parsons, 1920 a, p. 66; White, 1925, p. 39) or to (3) ceremonial stones placed on altars (Parsons, 1920, pp. 118-119; Boas, 1928, pt. 1, p. 39; Fewkes, 1902, p. 489; Stephen, 1936, p. 745, fig. 332, pl. 17). (p. 46)

[101] Yu'mahaia is the warrior of the south in Sia cosmology (Stevenson, 1894, p. 130). (p. 46)

[102] The Shiwana tcaianyi are the ones who treat lightning shock in Acoma today (White, 1932, p. 107). The Flint society is a witch-sickness curing society; it also has close associations with the O·pi, or Warriors' society (White, 1932, pp. 90, 107, ftn. 94). See also Bandelier, 1890, pp. 68-69, 385, for war functions of the Flint society.

Among eastern Keres the Flint society is very closely associated with the Koshari (White, 1935, p. 54P 1932 a, p. 41; Goldfrank, 1927, p. 143). (p. 50)

[103] see white 1932, pls. 11 and 12. (p. 50)

[104] Kiva walls are painted on First Mesa, at Isleta, and from early days in Jeddito Valley and elsewhere. (p. 50)

[105] Informant's note: They paint anything they want to get power from. Next time there might be other paintings [i. e., they change the designs for any ceremony]. (p. 50)

[106] See White 1932, pl. 16; also pp. 133-34. Cf. Laguna (Boas, 1929, pt. 1; pp. 201-203; Parsons, 192.1, pp. 180-81). (p. 51)

[107] The informant did not know much about the Giant society, as the altar had been taken to another pueblo before he was born. (p. 52)

[108] pa·ck'ᵘ (Boas, 1928, pt. 2, p.338, l. 6); Backo (White, 1935, p. 159, ftn. 90). Cf. Spanish pascua, "festival." (p. 52)

[109] Informant's note: When Iatiku had instructed the people about the katsina, she said that they were sacred and were not to be imitated in any way. (p. 52)

[110] Nevertheless, it is the dance now held in honor of the patron saint of Acoma, San Estevan.
(p. 52)

[111] At Santa Ana, Koshari or Kwiraina, usually the former, have charge of the feast for the saint (cf. Parsons, 1923 c). It is likely that this picture prevails at other Keresan pueblos. (p. 53)

[112] Informant's note: The drum invokes and wakes up the Clouds and the rain and cheers the people. Drums can be heard 10 miles or more. The drummer is a special man classed apart from the dancers. Drummers must care for the drums, keep them painted, and dry them before the ceremony. The drum is taken good care of

always. The drummer remains continent 4 days before a dance. As soon as they start making the new songs, the drummer must observe the purge. They think if you don't beat a drum with a good heart you get paralyzed. If you have the right heart, the drum will be light, otherwise it will be heavy and your arm will get numb. (p. 53)

[113] The informant said that this dance "had nothing to do with getting min or any purpose other than pleasure." Although this dance is now held at Acoma on September 2nd, Saint Stephen's day, the tradition states that it should be held about harvest time.
For dances In honor of patron saints in Keresan pueblos: White, 1932, pp. 102-106; Bourke, 1884, pp. 10-53 (for the dance at Santo Domingo which Bourke witnessed in 1881); White, 1935, pp. 159-160; Parsons, 1923 c; Bandelier, 1890 a, 136 ff.; Goldfrank, 1923. (p. 54)

[114] This is the "kicking game," generally called the kick stick race. See White, 1942; Parsons, 1923, p. 219; Culin, 1907, p. 668. (p. 54)

[115] See White, 1942. (p. 54)

[116] The informant stated at this point that there are five "society" kivas at Acorns. There are, he said, "two sacred chaianyi kivas; one is for medicine man, the other for Country Chief, religious and political."

The kiva question at Acorns is a perplexing one. Both Bandelier (1890, p. 268) and Mindeleff (1897, pp. 116, 207) state that there are six kivas at Acoma. This would coincide with the 6-kiva system of Zuñi, a kiva for each of the six directions. But White's informants stated (White, 1932, pp. 30-31) that there were five kivas, one for each of the five katsina dancing groups. Then there is Mauharots, the "head estufa [kiva]," which is the chamber for the cacique and the Antelope clan. Then there is the ceremonial chamber of the Fire society, also called k'a·'latc', as are the other six. Thus, at Acoma, there are seven chambers which are designated by the word k'a·'latc', kiva.

Since the Antelope clan, of which the cacique is the head, is the "head of the katsinas; the cacique being the father of the katsinas," it seems reasonable to include Mauharots as one of the six kivas associated with the katcina cult, The Fire society chamber, on the other hand, belongs to an entirely different cult and organization. Thus it seems justifiable to say that "Acoma has six kivas." But what the informant means here by "one religious and one political" kiva is hard to say. It seems likely that the Fire society's chamber is the "religious" kiva--the one for the medicine man. And, perhaps, Mauharots is the "political" kiva, for the war chief, since be is initiated there and reports to this kiva after returning from his night trips to rings (White, 1932, pp. 45-50).--L. A. W. (p. 55)

[117] Informant's note: Neshăats, "strength, power," nikunăts, "to get power, to prop up, to brace." (p. 55)

[118] The game is played today at Santo Domingo during Eastertide (Goggin, 1940). Possibly it was played on First Mesa in Stephen's day, although he did not see it or learn the significance of the miniature implements be describes as used in Niman Kachina (Stephen, 1936, pp. 529, 570, 573, figs. 320-322). (p. 55)

[119] Informant's note: In the court 2 stakes are placed about 6 inches apart, Just wide enough apart to let the ball pass through. The players stand about 75 feet away. They use a broad stick [cf. Stephen, 1936, fig. 320] or paddle, which is from 12 to 16 inches, to shove the ball. Two men play. each has 2 balls and 1 paddle. The game is to roll the ball between the stakes. (p. 55)

[120] Cf. White, 1932, p. 145. (p. 57)

[121] Cf. Santo Domingo (White, 1935, p. 200). (p. 57)

[122] There is an important katsina mask at Santo Domingo and at Santa Ana called Tsaiyaityuwitsa (White, 1935, pp. 97, 107, 172, fig. 22). (p. 58)

[123] Tsaiyaityuwit is a stereotyped picture of a Keresan hero--modest, quiet, unassuming, virtuous, thrifty,--a good hunter, living alone with his mother, a man able to influence the gods and to save the people. (p. 58)

[124] At Santo Domingo, spectators are not allowed to leave the plaza during a masked dance for any reason. (White, 1942). (p. 60)

[125] This is not my impression. Although it is true that officers and priests are not infrequently pictured in myths as powerless to bring rain, or wicked, and although it is not infrequently a "common man" who saves the day in mythology, I have received the distinct impression that the people place their trust in their priests and officers and their fetishes. If they can do nothing, there is little that a sicti (common person) can do.--L. A. W. (p. 60)

[126] See White, 1932, pp. 148-50. (p. 61)

[127] This is the first statement that Antelope chief was a medicine man. The cacique (Antelope chief) at Acoma recently was not a medicine man (While, 1932, pp. 41-42) (p. 62)

[128] A hint here of purgatory; the whole paragraph has a Catholic tone: punishment, penance, confession, prayer for somebody. Nor is "soul" (see below) a term generally used by Pueblos. (p. 65)

[129] Cf. White 1932, p. 137; also White, 1942. At Laguna the deceased had their faces painted with their respective clan designs (Parsons, 1923, p. 216); the shaman "will make [the deceased] so that he may be recognized" (Boas, 1928, pt. 1. p. 203). Common people at Sia are not painted at death, but "official members of cult societies" are painted (Stevenson, 1894, p. 144). The same practice is observed at Santa Ana (White, ms.) and at Cochiti (Goldfrank, 1927, p. 65). At Santo Domingo the deceased are said to be unpainted (White, 1935, p. 85), and there is no mention of face painting at San Felipe (White, 1932 a, pp. 60-61).
Apparently face painting of common people at death is practiced only at Laguna and Acoma. (p. 66)

[130] Informant's note: Women have their hair cut like Iatiku with hair parted to represent the Milky Way over the forehead, and cut with four corners to represent the ceremonial 4-day period. This is done so Iatiku will recognize them. The face is painted yellow with pollen to indicate a female. The red spots are fox looks; they point thus when dressed up for the dance. Necklace, because Iatiku wears one. Downy eagle feather in hair. (See White, 1942.)

A chaianyi is prepared as for a ceremony. The bangs are drawn up in a topknot. The black and white face Paint was prescribed by Iatiku. (Chaianyi work at night so they can see far like an owl.) The two chin, stripes are made by scratching away the paint. The turkey feathers at sides of head are painted green. Bear-claw necklace; arrowhead represents heart.

The ordinary man is painted with the red stripes of warrior or hunter. His haircut also represents the Milky Way. Abalone pendant. The feathers are chiutika [sparrow hawk, ctc'oTika', Boas, 1928, pt. 1, pp. 292-293]. Every man kills one, spreads out the tail feathers, and keeps them to be used when he dies. The corn husk in his hair shows he belongs to Iatiku, he has been initiated into the katsina. [Katsina initiates are referred to as G'uiraina (White, 1932, p. 71, ftn. 57) although this Keresan society is not found at Acoma. Elsewhere the sparrow-hawk feather is used by this society. At Laguna this society was closely associated With the katsina. Possibly the society once functioned at Acorns and possibly the dead wear sparrow, hawk feathers to indicate that they are to become katsina. On First Mesa and at the Laguna colony at Isleta deceased adult males are arrayed as katsina.--E. C. P.) (p. 66)

[131] Cf. Acoma (White, 1932, pp. 137-38; Parsons, 1918, pp. 176-180; White, 1942). Laguna (Parsons, 1920, pp. 128-29; 1923, pp. 216-19; Boas, 1928, pt. 1, pp. 203-204). Santo Domingo (White, 1935, pp. 83-87). San Felipe (White, 1932 a, pp. 60-61). Sia (Stevenson, 1894, pp. 143-46). Cochiti (Dumarest, 1919, pp. 166-170; Goldfrank, 1922, pp. 65-66). (p. 66)

[132] Here and elsewhere, the informant appears to use the term "forget" where the ethnologist would say "exorcise" or "cleanse," or, as Spanish Indians elsewhere would say, "limpiarse." (p. 66)

[133] Informant's note: This groove in the rock Iatiku made when she was abandoned by her sister. She performed the ceremony in order to forget. Later Iatiku taught people to perform the ceremony in order to forget whatever they wished, including the dead. (Cf. Parsons, 1923, p. 258.) At Laguna a pebble was shoved along a similar figure cut into the rock; but here the ritual was for prognostication in sickness. If the pebble slips from under the foot, the patient will die. (p. 66)

[134] According to others, the arrow point is returned to the relatives. (p. 66)

[135] Tsa·'lts. This word is also used for "soul." (p. 66)

[136] I have never succeeded in uncovering among the Keres any "bad words" except witch, kanadyaiya and "evil spirit," croadyam.--L. A. W. (p. 67)

[137] It is a common Pueblo notion that, if one does not observe ritual rules faithfully, he is likely to sicken and perhaps die. (p. 67)

[138] Cf. White, 1932, pp. 71-75. (p. 68)

[139] Informant's note: On some occasions when the katsina come to Acoma there will be a group of 20 or so of the same kind. Nowadays there are many kivas and each one will represent only one kind at a time, or perhaps two. Sometimes, if it is necessary to have more masks, they may borrow them from another kiva. At Acoma all masks are kept in kiva and maybe taken out only for ceremonies. Masks are not the property of individuals. [Members of the kachina organization at Zuñi own dance masks, but nowhere among Keres is there individual ownership of masks.] Masks are kept in a room, plastered shut [in the custody either of kiva chiefs or of medicine men]. There are four rooms in Acoma kivas; three of them are plastered up. The kivas in Acoma have altars [Mauharots is probably one of them, perhaps the chamber of the Fire society is the other. See previous note on Acoma kivas, p. 45). The chaianyi keeps the altar in his own house, fits it up for ceremonies. (p. 71)

[140] Informant's note: Today they dance 10 times before noon. (p. 71)

[141] At Acoma today the masked dancers eat outdoors, but behind the church (White, 1932, p. 83). At Santo Domingo and at San Felipe the masked dancers eat in a house set aside for them. All spectators, especially women and children, must go indoors. Old women bring food to the war chief's helpers who take it to the dancers (White, 1935, pp. 96-97; White, 1932 a, p. 39). (p. 71)

[142] Cf. White, 1932, p. 87. (p. 72)

[143] Informant's note: "The masks used for katsina impersonation are the same that are used for the Kopishtaiya; they are merely painted and decorated differently." [See White, 1932, p. 8, b, and pl. 10, a.] (p. 74)

[144] Laguna Gomaiowish masks have knobs on them containing seeds. The informant must be confusing Kopishtaiya masks here with Gomaiowish masks, for the former have not been reported from Laguna or, indeed, from any other Keresan pueblo. (p. 74)

[145] Cf. p. 16. (p. 74)

[146] Cf. White, 1032, pp. 85-88; Boas, 1928, pt. 1, p. 201. (p. 74)

[147] The cacique (Antelope chief) at Acorns today tells initiates into the katsina organization "everything about the katsina" (White, 1932, pp. 74-75). (p. 76)

[148] There are five katsina dance groups at Acoma. There is no "Kachina society" as at Zuñi. (p. 76)

[149] Informant's note: Maati is the span of thumb and forefinger. Four maati was the old way of saying "far"; the modern word is teetsa. (p. 80)

[150] Probably ha·'yactc'ιTcunʸi hɑ'tc'tcTse, Whirlwind old man (cf. Boas, 1928, pt. 2, p. 190, ll. 19, 26). (p. 81)

[151] This is the rite observed by other Pueblos and by Navaho on a journey. It is South American practice also. There, among Andean peoples, the sticks or stones are left in a pile. (p. 82)

[152] The impersonator of the Kopishtaiya draws four lines on the ground with a flint between himself and his mask at the conclusion of the ceremony (White, 1932, p. 87). This is a common Pueblo way of separating one's self from something sacred or injurious. (p. 82)

[153] Informant's note: This method of getting rid of disease is still followed. When another village is visited the visitor on leaving brushes sickness off and leaves it behind. No sand painting is used. (p. 82)

[154] Cf. White, 1932, p. 145. Stevenson renders wash'pa "cactus" (Stevenson, 1894, p. 19); Bandelier, "buffalo grass" [Bulbilis dactyloides] (Bandelier, 1940, vol. 2, p. 216); a Sia informant identified it with the Spanish chamiso or saltbush (Afriplex canescens) (White, ms.). Saltbush is commonly called "sagebrush" by many, especially newcomers, in the Southwest. Cŭkŭ means "corner," as in koamicŭkŭ, "southeast corner," the winter solstice (White, 1932, p. 85). (See Washpa, Washpashuka, in Handbook of American Indians.) (p. 82)

[155] Cf. White, 1932, p. 79, pl. 2, c, pp. 94-96; 1942: Represented at Acoma today by a boy about 10 years 1932, p. 94). He carries a little pottery canteen and a firebrand. (p. 83)

[156] Cf. White, 1932, p. 79; 1942. (p. 84)

[157] Cf. White, 1922, pp. 94-96, pl. 2, b. (p. 84)

[158] For K'o·muDina, see White, 1932, pp. 94-96. (p. 84)

[159] The Keresan term is kokwi'mα. Gunn speaks of the Storoka as "koquima, or hermaphrodite" (Gunn, 1917, p.173). In the Kyanakwe ceremony of Zuñi, which has been equated with the Storoka, the kachina transvestite, Kothlama, appears. (See White, 1942.) (p. 84)

[160] Cf. White, 1932, pp. 88-94. No other Keresan pueblo has this ceremony so far as is known. (p. 85)

[161] House. See p. 88. (p. 85)

[162] A sheep, today (see White, 1932, p. 89). (p. 86)

[163] I am reminded of the interbarrio or interhacienda fiesta fighting of Mexico or Ecuador.--E. C. (p. 86)

[164] This ceremony was not held every year, but every 5 or 6 years (White, 1922, p. 88.) (p. 87)

[165] The Antelope people paint themselves pink all over their bodies; their faces are painted with ya'katca (reddish brown) and with stcamu·n (black, sparkling) put on

over the red under their eyes. The house of Antelope clan (or cacique's house) at Acoma is pink, too (White, 1932, pp. 42-43, 91). (p. 87)

[166] "This [blood] is a sacrifice to the earth" (White, 1932, p. 92). Compare the belief that rooster blood, spilled in the "chicken pull," is "good for rain" (White, 1932, p. 106). (p. 89)

[167] Informant's note: The name of this ceremony was kaiyapaitsaneetya, "come to club"; but it is now called kauwastheetya "attacking" (Cf. White, 1932, pp. 77, 88.) (p. 89)

[168] Ants cause sores on the body and sore throat according to general Keresan belief. (See White, 1930, pp. 607-608.) (p. 90)

[169] No Ant medicine society has been reported from Acoma, though "there used to be an Ant society" there (White, 1932, p. 107). There were Ant societies at Sia (Stevenson, 1894, pp. 69, 104) and at Laguna (Parsons, 1920, p. 109, Ito. 3). An Ant shaman from Zuñi lived in Santo Domingo for many years; he died in 1932. He practiced curing, not only in Santo Domingo, but in Santa Ana, Sia, San Felipe, Cochiti, and perhaps in some Tewa pueblos (White, 1935, pp. 67-68; 1932 a, p. 40; Parsons, 1923 a, p. 492). (p. 91)

[170] See Stevenson, 1894, p. 100, for the extraction of ants from the body of a sick Sia boy. But it was the Giant society that did this, not the Ant. (p. 91)

[171] (2) The "ants" which Stevenson saw extracted at Sia were "tiny pebbles." (p. 91)

[172] Flint is a "form of lightning," according to Keresan belief; one can strike lightning sparks from flint, therefore it contains lighting. The association of flint with lightning and thunder is, of course, a widespread idea not only in the Now World but in the Old World also.
(p. 93)

[173] Keresan informants invariably use the English word "work" to designate the exercise, or manipulation of supernatural power. (p. 93)

[174] The Keresan name for Laguna. The Informant is translating from Spanish, not from Keresan. (p. 94)

[175] Actually at Laguna there is a grooved rock for pebble pushing (Parsons, 1923, fig. 20). For Zuñi see Parsons, 1923, figs. 21, 22; Benedict, 1935, vol. 1, p. 117. (p. 94)

[176] Cf. White, 1932, p. 145. (p. 94)

[177] Cf. White, 1932, p. 26. (p. 95)

[178] At Cochiti and Jemez the women in this dance form an inner circle. (p. 96)

[179] A great virtue among the Pueblos. (p. 96)

[180] See White, 1942. (p. 96)

[181] This is not a Pueblo Indian conception; the father is not "the head of the family." This informant, who had left Acoma and who wanted to adopt white man's ways. was, however, unquestionably the head of his family. (p. 98)

[182] Apparently not because they cared about their destination but because they had lost the parrots. (p. 98)

[183] Cf. Acoma, White, 1942; Santo Domingo, White, 1935, pp. 187-191; Zuñi, Parsons, 1923 b, 155-159. (p. 100)

[184] An Acoma man was sent to the penitentiary at Santa Fé to serve a long term for murder. When he returned to Acoma he said that what he suffered most while in prison was being pursued his sleep by ko'ok.--L. A. W. (p. 100)

[185] White, 1932, pp. 97-101; Boas, 1928, pt. 1, pp. 2891-90. See White, 1942. (p. 102)

[186] The informant said that this term includes the rulers of the directions, the katsina and others. White was told that ckau'pictaiya is a term embracing the spirits of the four directions, Sun, Moon, Wind, and Earth, but that it does not include the katsina, Lightning, or Iatiku. He was unable to ascertain the basis of this distinction (p. 103).

[187] Informant's note: At Acoma one could become an Opi [a member of the Warriors' society] only by killing a human enemy, but in other places one could become Opi through killing an eagle or a bear. Cf. White, 1932, p. 96 At Santa Ana one could become an Opi through killing a bear, puma, and perhaps wildcat and eagle (White, ms.). (p. 104)

[188] Mo'acomi does not mean enemies literally, but "nomadic Indian tribes adjacent to the pueblos:" Navaho, Apache, Ute, Comanche. Actually, of course, they were enemies of the pueblos. Cf. Gunn, 1917, p. 86. "The Queres call the Navajos 'Moashrum.' The name means, 'those who came out of the hills or rough country.'" (p. 104)

[189] This sentence seems highly paraphrased or highly acculturated for: This is the way you are to dance when you take a scalp (or have killed an enemy). See below. (p. 105)

[190] According to Boas, 1928, pt. 1, pp. 16, 207, 286, 289, the woman who dances with Masewi in the scalp dance is ko'oko, and is the sister of the War Twins, not their mother. (p. 106)

[191] Cf. White, 1935, p. 60, ftn. 56. (p. 106)

[192] Cf. White, 1942. (p. 107)

[193] Masewi and Oyoyewi live under a rock (or perhaps two rocks) on top of the Acoma mesa, east of the village (White, 1932, fig. 1, pp. 30, 146). (p. 107)

[194] Obviously a paraphrase, but for what? (p. 107)

[195] See White, 1932, pp. 147, 172-180; 1942. (p. 108)

[196] There are two great natural reservoirs on top of the Acoma mesa (White, 1932, p. 29). (p. 108)

[197] Yaka, "corn," Kotona is the completely kernelled ear of corn used ceremonially. The meaning of kanach is obscure. ka is his, or her; perhaps nach is head-- nack'a'inyi is head at Santa Ana. The great rock-mesa upon which Acoma pueblo rests is referred to ceremonially as a kotona, "standing erect"; the people live upon the kotona's head (White, 1942) (p. 108)

[198] There are several of these Ocatc Paiyatyamo, anthropomorphic sun gods, brothers, who live at Sunrise Place. Each day one of them takes the sun across the heavens.--L. A. W. (p. 110)

[199] Ho·ctya·'ka (bow); k'acT^{y}a·'tsi (rainbow).--L. A W. (p. 111)

[200] Acoma hunters pray to the Sun to help them (White, 1932, p. 102). (p. 111)

[201] Variant: "There are lots of cko·yo [giants] roaming around this country," she would tell them, might catch you and eat you." "Oh, we're not afraid!" the boys would say.--L. A. W. (p. 112)

[202] The war god twins in a Sia myth skinned a bear's paws (Stevenson, 1894, p. 47). See also White, 1942, for an account of a medicine man skinning a bear. (p. 112)

[203] Variant: In the west den were wolves that are always hungry, in the south den, snakes. some of them rattlesnakes. "The Twins made pets of the snakes, too. When the Paiyatyamos came back they found the rattlesnakes crawling around the boys' necks and faces and not hurting them at all.".--L. A. W. (p. 114)

[204] See p. 24. (p. 114)

[205] Variant: When the Twins stood up with their father the other "Sun Youths tried to pick their own brother out from among the three, but they looked so much alike they could not do it. Finally they said, "All right! These boys are your sons!" (p. 115)

[206] Each officer in a Keresan pueblo has a little staff, a stick or cane of office, called ya·'Bi (White, 1932, p. 129, 4, 4, c; 1935, pp. 38, 47). (p. 115)

[207] The War chiefs are allowed anywhere, in any ceremony, in the pueblo. (p. 115)

[208] Informant's note: The pouch (koskatuna) contains ant gravel and a few hairs from scalps. The gravel keeps away the disease and bad luck that the hair might carry. A fighting ant never goes back, and is very strong. (The Ant chaianyi uses a bat dried out. The bat is laid on the ant hill. The ants eat the flesh of the bat, then they grow wings and fly away.) (p. 115)

[209] Cf. White, 1932, pp. 60-61. (p. 118)

[210] According to White, 1932, pp. 42, 60, it is the cacique, the head of the Antelope Clan, who appoints the officers. (p. 118)

[211] Cf. White, 1942. (p. 118)

[212] Antelope nawai (head man) is the cacique. It is curious that he is always referred to by this informant as Antelope Man; he is usually designated "cacique," at least in talking to white people. (p. 118)

[213] Cf. White, 1932, p. 45. According to White: First war chief is Cutimïti; second, Cpatimïti; third, Maiyatcotimïti; then there are three cook-helpers, and ten "little chiefs" as assistants. (p. 119)

[214] See Plan (fig. 1). (See White, 1942.) (p. 119)

[215] Keres use "luck" equivalent to "blessing." (p. 120)

[216] Cf. White, 1932, pp. 52-55. (p. 120)

[217] A colony of Acoma, to the northwest, located on the Santa Fé railroad and the main automobile highway between Albuquerque and Gallup. (p. 121)

[218] Cf. White, 1932, p. 52. (p. 122)

[219] Of. White, 1932, p. 45. (p. 122)

[220] Informant's note: The Mountain prayer sticks are the largest made, over a foot long. The twigs and leaves are the clothes of the prayer sticks. [In other prayer sticks, feathers somewhat similarly placed are called the clothes.] (p. 123)

[221] Cf. White, 1932, pp. 46-51. (p. 124)

[222] Gotsicpawatsa, "Pretty Spring." (p. 124)

[223] See White, 1932 p. 129. (p. 124)

[224] The communal farming is usually said by Keres to be done for the cacique (White, 1932, p. 42; Boas, 1928, pt. 1, p. 288; White, 1932 a, p. 14; 1935, p. 35; Dumarest, 1919, p. 197; Goldfrank, 1927, pp. 40, 93-94). But White (1942) also reports that a communal farm at Acoma is worked for the War (or Country) Chief-- at least he has charge of it. This is probably not an instance of two different customs but different ways of reporting the same custom: the fields are worked, probably for the cacique, but are tended under the direction of the War Chief.--L. A. W. (p. 125)

[225] See White, 1932, pp. 48-50; 1942. (p. 125)

[226] See p. 81. (p. 125)

[227] The informant was once in American vaudeville. (p. 127)

[228] See p. 48. Kapina chaianyi represents Tiamuni, Iatiku's "husband." (p. 127)

[229] Into the other feathers bundled around the fetish. (p. 127)

[230] According to White 1932, p. 40, the two under war chiefs may refuse, but the first chief must drink it. (p. 128)

[231] Cf. White, 1932, pp. 71-75; 1942. (p. 129)

[232] Women at Acoma are not initiated into the societies (Informant). Although Acoma women are initiated to the Katsina society, they never wear masks (White,

1932, p. 70). At Sia, according to Stevenson, women participate in masked dances, presumably wearing masks (Stevenson, 1894, p. 116). White's Sia informants stated that women were initiates into the katsina organization, but declared positively that they never wore masks (White, ms.). At Santa Ana some women are admitted to the katsina organization and may wear katsina masks representing females (White, ms.). At Santo Domingo and San Felipe women are not admitted to the katsina organization; moreover, theoretically, at least, they are kept in ignorance of the fact that the katsina dancers are men (White, 1935, pp. 49, 83, 96-97, 101, 104; 1932 a, pp. 27, 35). At Cochiti, women are kept in ignorance of the identity of the katsina dancers (Dumarest, 1919, pp. 174-175; see also Goldfrank, 1927 pp. 44 104). (p. 129)

[233] Does this imply that the clan has a stock of personal names, like the Hopi clan? For Hopi-Acoma parallels, several drawn from this monograph, see Parsons 1939, pp. 980-982. (p. 129)

[234] Cf. White, 1932, p. 30. (p. 130)

[235] The house of the cacique who is Antelope clan nawai. (p. 130)

[236] Informant's note: The hair is tied in between, with a cotton string. Cf. hair frame of Hopi maiden. (p. 132)

[237] Included in this plate are "prayer sticks in the form of pins (otsatiatni) for fastening a woman's mantle. These prayer sticks are made and deposited by Koshari." (Cf. Parsons, 1918 a, pl. 3). (p. 132)

[238] First Mesa Hopi say to their children, "The crows are coming wearing yellow stockings," which means there is to be a kachina dance.--E. C. P. No connection is made between crows and kachina among eastern Keres.--L. A. W. (p. 132)

[239] Cf. White, 1932, pp. 97-101. (p. 134)

[240] see White, 1942. (p. 134)

[241] The cotton-wrapped, bead- and feather-decked corn ear fetish of the Keresan curing society. See Acoma (White, 1932, p. 129); Sia (Stevenson, 1894, p. 4k,, ftn. 1, l. 9); Laguna (Parsons, 1920, pp. 95-96); Santo Domingo (White, 1935, p. 161); Cochiti (Dumarest, 1919, p. 155). It represents the mother of the Indians, Iatiku, and is also called yaya, "mother." Among eastern Keres it is called ia'riko. Honani is the Hopi word for badger, although the accent is different: Acoma, ho'nani; Hopi, hona'ni. (p. 161)

[242] The cotton-wrapped, bead- and feather-decked corn ear fetish of the Keresan curing society. See Acoma (White, 1932, p. 129); Sia (Stevenson, 1894, p. 4k,, ftn. 1, l. 9); Laguna (Parsons, 1920, pp. 95-96); Santo Domingo (White, 1935, p. 161); Cochiti (Dumarest, 1919, p. 155). It represents the mother of the Indians, Iatiku, and is also called yaya, "mother." Among eastern Keres it is called ia'riko. Honani is the Hopi word for badger, although the accent is different: Acoma, ho'nani; Hopi, hona'ni (p. 162).

www.ingramcontent.com/pod-product-compliance
Lightning Source LLC
Chambersburg PA
CBHW051545010526
44118CB00022B/2590